CHROMA SUTRA

The Holland Lectures on

Color Theory for Artists

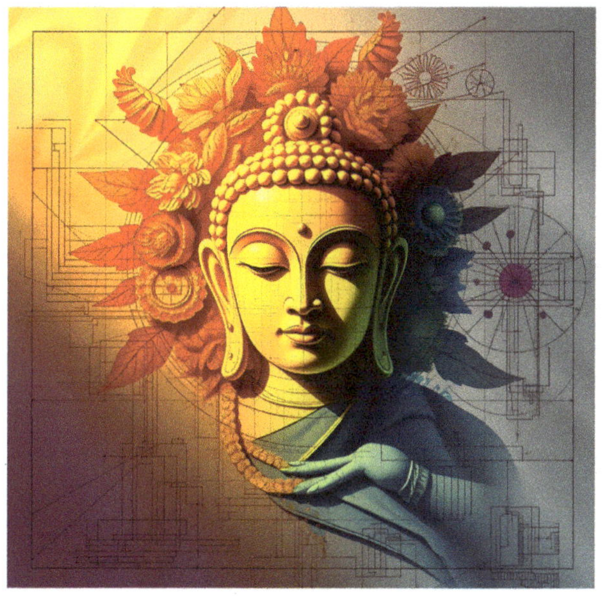

(A Grand Unified Theory of Color for Artists and Scientists)

Walter Holland

Edited by Michael Moralis

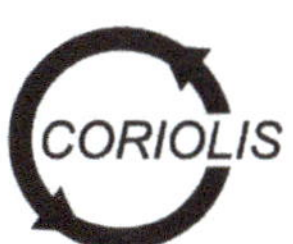

Print ISBN: 979-8-218-84180-5

Book Cover by Coriolis Staff

www.coriolisrecords.com

Illustrations by Walter Holland

First edition 2025

Preface

Color theory seems simple enough. The reality is that it's confusing. Particularly for someone who paints, because it can be a marriage of art and science, and science is often intimidating for creative people. This book is meant to make you comfortable with certain aspects of science as they apply to art. But there are laws and rules that govern science, and it helps if you know them. Art is more flexible and individualistic; as you learn, you discover what rules you can disregard. But the more you learn, the more complicated it gets until you reach a point when you understand color theory without thinking about it.

The best way to think about color is that it is the result of the interaction of light, the eye, and the human brain. But that's complicated and often intimidating. And it doesn't help much when mixing paint. Color wheels are supposed to help, but inaccuracies and ambiguities about colors complicate it again, just when you thought you were starting to understand color theory and the role of primary and complementary colors. That's progress!

Science and vocabulary both evolve. For example, the term cyan came into use to describe a color (cyan blue) in the late 1800s. The term "indigo" was used in English as far back as about 1289, referring to a dark blue color derived from a plant found in the Indus Valley of India. So cyan and indigo moved into the English language, referring to distinctive shades of blue. A purplish-red aniline (derived from coal tar) dye was invented in

1859 by French chemist François-Emmanuel Verguin. He initially called the color "fuchsine," named for fuchsia flowers. It was renamed as magenta to commemorate Napoleon's victory at the Battle of Magenta, fought between France and Austria in 1859. Magenta is a non-spectral color, meaning it cannot be generated by a single wavelength of light. Instead, it is a result of the combination of red and blue light wavelengths.

It is important to understand that a major reason students have trouble with color theory is a conflict between the Enlightenment or Age of Reason and Romanticism. Both were philosophical movements during the 18th and 19th centuries. The Enlightenment emphasized reason, logic and scientific inquiry. Romanticism was a backlash. The color wheel came into existence in the midst of this tension.

NEWTON, GOETHE AND ITTEN

Sir Isaac Newton was a mathematician, physicist and astronomer. He discovered a lot of things, including gravity. But beginning in 1665 and 1666, he began studying sunlight, using a prism. He discovered that shining sunlight through a prism caused the "white light" to bend and yield the seven colors of the rainbow: red, orange, yellow, green, blue, indigo, and violet, referred to as ROYGBIV. This "visible" spectrum was a scientific approach to color. Since Newton's time, indigo was replaced in the general vocabulary by blue. Newton presented the continuum as a color wheel (or color circle or color disk).

Advancements in science and technology determined that the visible colors occupy a segment of the electromagnetic radiation spectrum (EMS). The EMS also includes non-visible wavelengths: radio, gamma and microwaves. We're talking about colors, though. The fovea of the retina of human eye contains specialized cells (cones) that are photoreceptors. The cones convert light into signals in the brain, allowing us to see colors in the visible spectrum. There are three kinds of cones, sensitive to the colors red, green and blue.

In 1704 in England, Newton published *Opticks, or A treatise of the reflections, refractions, inflections and colours of light*. Since Newton's time, many things have evolved, including the English vocabulary, not to mention science and color wheels.

But Newton was a scientist. Johann Wolfgang von Goethe was not; he was a German Romantic. Best known as a philosopher and poet, he was also a painter and draftsman. Almost a century after Newton, Goethe – a key figure in the German Romantic period – developed his own theories about light, focusing on the psychological effects that colors have on people. He approached color as more of a Romantic than Newton. Goethe followed in the footsteps of Aristotle, who wrote that color was the interplay of light and darkness. Almost a century after Newton's work – which met with passionate opposition over time in many quarters – Goethe focused on the mood evoked by various colors.

Johannes Itten (1888-1967) was a Swiss teacher, expressionist painter and color theorist. Initially trained as an elementary teacher, he became one of the first people to work at the famed Bauhaus school of design, architecture and applied arts, and when he joined the school in 1919 he was appointed as a Master. He was responsible for the mandatory introductory or preliminary courses (known as Vorkurs).

After abandoning elementary school teaching, Itten studied under German painter Adolf Hölzel (1853-1934) who started out as a realist painter but became a champion of modern styles including abstractionism and impressionism. Itten created an elaborate framework for color theory derived in part on the work of the German Romantic artist and theorist Philippe Otto Runge, who developed a three-dimensional "color sphere" that was related to Goethe's color theory as well as that of Newton.

Itten is considered a minor deity in the world of color theory. And so he should be; but Itten was not a scientist, like Newton. He was a charismatic teacher and focused on bringing out students' intuition as well as love of discovery and learning. However, he was also a bit of a mystic, and more of a Romantic than a scientist. This clashed with the Modernist approach of Bauhaus founder Walter Gropius (1883-1969), architect-director of the school, leading to Itten's departure. In his 1961 books, The Elements of Color and The Art of Color, he captured ideas originally presented in his courses.

Itten had developed a "color star," but then transformed that into a color wheel. In his books, Itten explored dyads, triads and tetrads (harmonious combinations of two, three or four colors which could be identified by imposing geometric shapes on his color wheel, which consisted of 12 colors (including blue and red, not cyan and magenta) to help identify complementary colors. The topic of primary and complementary colors can be a source of confusion to art students and artists. Even color theorists can be baffled by subtle nuances.

COLOR WHEELS AND PRIMARY COLORS

Color Wheels (also called color circles or color disks) are tools that supposedly make it easier to determine primary and complementary colors. Unfortunately for artists, they have about 300 years of history. And what was believed be true 50 or 100 or 300 years ago just isn't accurate, even though it may have been printed in a book. For example, Newton's prism experiments revealed the seven colors of the rainbow, and his book was illustrated with a diagram of a seven-color wheel.

Primary colors are three core colors that supposedly can't be made by mixing or blending with other colors. However, they can be mixed in varying proportions to make all other colors. The primary colors are the building blocks of a color system. What is traditionally taught starting in elementary school is that the primary colors are red, yellow and blue (RYB).

The trouble is that the primary colors vary, depending on some key factors such as whether they are intended for use in additive or subtractive systems. Conventional wisdom is that the primary colors are Red, Yellow and Blue (RYB). That's what traditional color wheels that are sold commercially tell you. However, this is not correct.

Part of what has happened is that there are two different systems and they happen to use different primary colors, which affects the complementary colors. Newton based his observations on light. But when using light, the primary colors are Red, Green and Blue (RGB). So "in reality," the primary colors are Red, Green and Blue! But reality is as tricky as color theory. For printing, the primary colors are Cyan, Magenta and Yellow (CMY). Look at the inks in a computer printer, which can produce any color!

THE WAY THE EYE SEES COLOR

The normal human eye perceives color when white light – the visual spectrum – stimulates cone cells in the fovea (an area of the retina). The three types of cone cells are photoreceptors sensitive to specific bands of wavelengths on the visible light spectrum. Cone cells allow us to see color. The 3 types of cone cells found in the retina are L (red), M (green), and S (blue) cones. This diversity in sensitivity allows for the perception of a wide range of colors through the combination of signals from these photoreceptors.

CONCLUSION

Above all, this book answers questions that are not easy to even formulate until you've absorbed and processed a lot of information and misinformation about colors and color theory. It clarifies errors, inaccuracies and ambiguities about color wheels, and presents a new and improved one for art students, artists, instructors and color theorists.

This book will demystify the specialized vocabulary of the art world, clarifying terms such as hue, saturation and value, or tints, tones and shades, explaining the differences and distinctions. It is a bridge between science and art. It presents leading-edge science and some new or updated laws for color theory. It also includes an indispensable new and improved color wheel that art students, artists, and instructors should use to simplify their lives and work.

It may seem technical at times, but the plan is definitely not to turn you into a physicist or biologist. The goal is to make you a more informed, more effective and less frustrated artist.

Michael Moralis

Table of Contents

Chapter 1
Introduction

If you are trained as an artist, you undoubtedly studied color theory while you were in art school. Unfortunately, you may have been done a tremendous disservice, because most likely, nearly everything you learned was either misleading or entirely untrue! There are at least two reasons for this: firstly, color theory is a multi-disciplinary and extremely complex subject, which is difficult to grasp in its entirety. In fact, the physiological mechanism by which we perceive color is not yet entirely understood, even as I write this. Secondly, most of what your instructors were taught was probably patently erroneous, and they were just passing that misinformation along to you.

If you go to any art supply store today and ask to buy a color wheel, they will sell you something that is completely wrong and misleading. To complicate matters further, the classic textbook, which has been considered the bible of color theory for artists for the last 50 years (Itten, The Elements of Color, 1970), contains many misconceptions, and theoretical and practical errors. I feel truly terrible having to attack the work of a minor deity such as Johannes Itten, but I believe we now have better pigments and better science that prove a lot of his conclusions to be incorrect. However, I still feel awful about contradicting such a revered teacher...which I cover in more detail in chapter 12, titled "Apologies to Professor Itten."

Given the above situation, it becomes clear why most artists find color theory to be one of the most difficult subjects to apply and thoroughly comprehend. Color theory as it has been taught is frequently a source of frustration for artists, particularly the areas of mixing paint and color harmony, (which frankly, can drive painters to drink). Don't despair: the parts of color theory that artists need to know aren't that complicated. You just need someone to show you the true path.

Reconciling Art and Physics

Color theory is a very broad field, finding application in virtually all aspects of everyday life. In fact, it would be very difficult for an individual to not be stimulated by color almost every waking minute. Diverse areas such as interior design and printed media, television, fabric design, automotive paint, advertising, architecture and food presentation, are all constantly bombarding us with sensations of color. Although each of these commercial fields is very different from the other, they have one thing in common: The science of color nowadays is extremely advanced.

Whether you are a chemist or a theater lighting technician, a television engineer or an optical designer or an optometrist, you are required to study and understand the physics of light and color. Did you notice that artist was not on that list? At some point in history, artists veered off of the path of scientific knowledge of color, presumably owing to the fact that artists work with pigments. Historically, pigments have been extremely limited in their ability to perform according to the expectations of one trained in color theory, so decisions were made to teach painters a version of color theory that was not remotely accurate, but one that sort of functions (however minimally) for people working with paints and pigments.

In essence, people who are technically or scientifically trained in color theory are taught one thing, and artists are taught something completely different. In my mind, this is a bit like living in Los Angeles and telling a child that the sky is blue, and having the child say: "but I can see that the sky is brown!" One approach is to insist that the sky is blue, until you are blue in the face. This is the manner in which artist's color theory is normally handled. But another method, and the method I find most appropriate in both situations, is to explain that in theory, and under certain conditions, the sky is blue. However, due to atmospheric pollutants and so on, the sky sometimes appears to be brown.

I feel that it is far more useful and rewarding for an artist to understand the behavior of light and color, and then to learn the limitations of colorants and pigments, and why and under what conditions they sometimes fall short of theoretical predictions. For an artist, there is nothing more rewarding than solving color problems intuitively. However, it is very comforting to know that in reserve, you have the theoretical knowledge to fall back on when intuition finds occasion to shortchange you.

The Scope of this Text

This book will present a series of ideas that may seem very foreign, contradictory and even absurd to those trained (or shall we say mis-trained), in traditional color theory for artists. I have not discovered any unknown or profound information. All of the ideas that I am presenting can be verified either empirically by experiment, or by examining any current technical text on the subject of light and color. The ideas that I am expounding are neither new, nor revolutionary except in this way: By correcting the artist's color wheel, I was able to see many new ideas and color relationships. Harmonies and laws that were heretofore obscured by the errors in the traditional color wheel became clear. The laws of primary colors and mathematical harmonic relationships became obviously apparent. These changes to the color wheel make color theory work for artists at last.

My goal for this book is to collect facts and ideas from many diverse areas of science and industry that have heretofore been off limits to painters and artists, and to present these concepts in a concise, easy to understand and practical manner. I am not attempting to address all areas of color theory, only those areas that somehow seem to have been neglected with respect to artists. One reason for this is that subjects such as color effects, (the interaction of two or more colors placed in proximity) and color contrasts, have already been expertly covered, and there is an abundance of good information available on the subject. Another reason is that as one follows color theory to the fringes of art, one enters the domains of psychology, physiology, neurology, physics and so on, and while these may be of interest to the artist, they are not prerequisites to being a skilled colorist.

This book is the culmination of my research and the color theory lectures I have given at various colleges and universities beginning in 1985 and continuing into the new millennium. Many of the illustrations are the same drawings I might have made on the chalkboard at the time of the lectures.

I would like to thank the following people for their support and encouragement during the years of research that this project required: Dr. Richard and Clara Watson, Professor William and Angie Boaz, Professor Susan Rankaitis, Professor Roy Montibon, Professor John Yules and Ellen Holland.

It fascinates me, in hindsight, that some of the most confounding problems throughout the study of color can be answered by looking closely at the results of Newton's original experiments performed in 1665-1666. I would suggest to anyone excited by the field of color, to read Newton (Newton, 1704), which is marvelous poetry, and to "procure himself a glass prisme" and repeat these experiments. Use the prism to break the sunlight into its component colors. Subtract any one of the colors and use a converging lens to combine the remaining colors making its complement. As you perform these historic experiments, ask yourself why yellow is such a bright color, why there is no magenta in the spectrum and why when you isolate any one color, its complement is so bright.

My hope is that this book will become a familiar and trusted friend that sits by your easel, giving reference and guidance and comforting you on your journey as an artist. So, with this in mind, let's regress to the elementary school level, and relearn the marvels of light and color. By the end of this journey, you will have earned membership to that most exclusive of clubs: artists who truly understand color.

CHROMA SUTRA

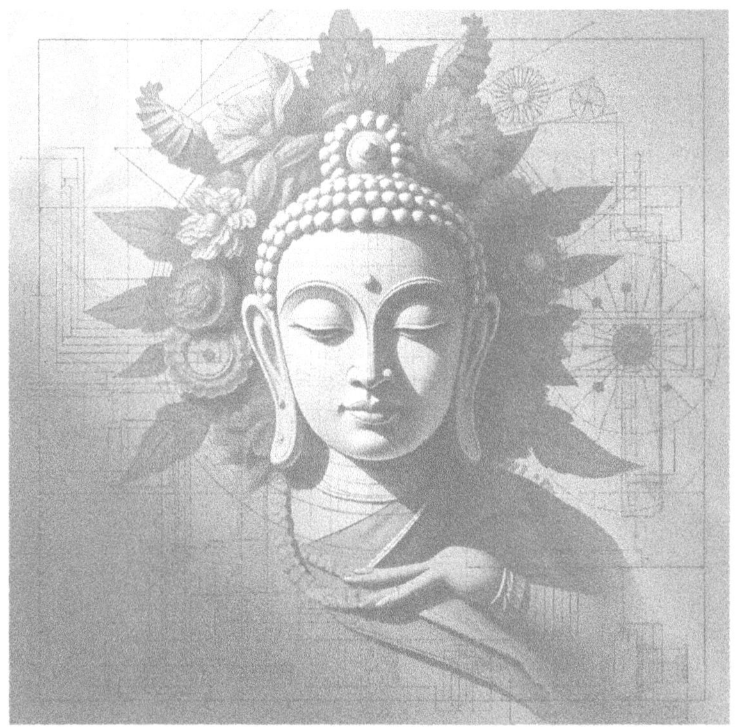

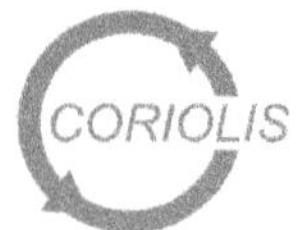

Chapter 2
What is Color?

The Perception of Color

A good place to begin the journey of understanding color is to ask yourself: What is color? Another way to ask that same question would be: How do we perceive color? At the time of this writing, the exact mechanism of color perception is not fully understood, however, we know that the process incorporates mechanisms and phenomenon involving the cones in the eye, wavelength, reflectance, absorption, pigments and colorants, illumination and so on. In addition, input from color receptors in the eye are further processed by the brain, leading to the extremely complex process of color perception. We can refine and simplify this list a bit, to distill the essential notion that color perception relies on a combination of three things: Illumination, an Object and an Observer.

Each of these three elements can cause a variation in the way that we perceive a given color sample. For example, a sample of color will vary dramatically when viewed in daylight and then viewed again under fluorescent lighting. Let's look at each of these three basic elements of color perception: illumination, object and observer individually, and in more detail, in order to understand how each element affects the color that we see and perceive.

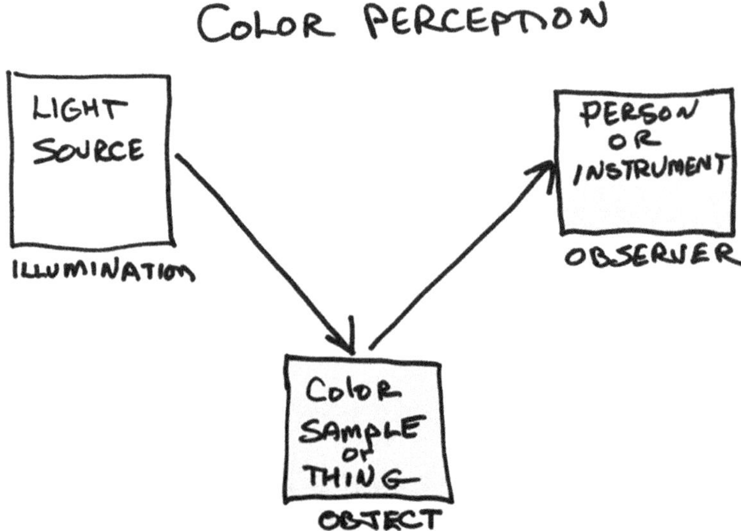

Figure 1. Observer, Object, Illumination

First, we'll examine the basic physiological mechanism of perception. As I mentioned above, the three essential requirements for color perception are a source of illumination, an object and an observer. Study the illustrations of figure 1 and 2, and you will see how this relationship works.

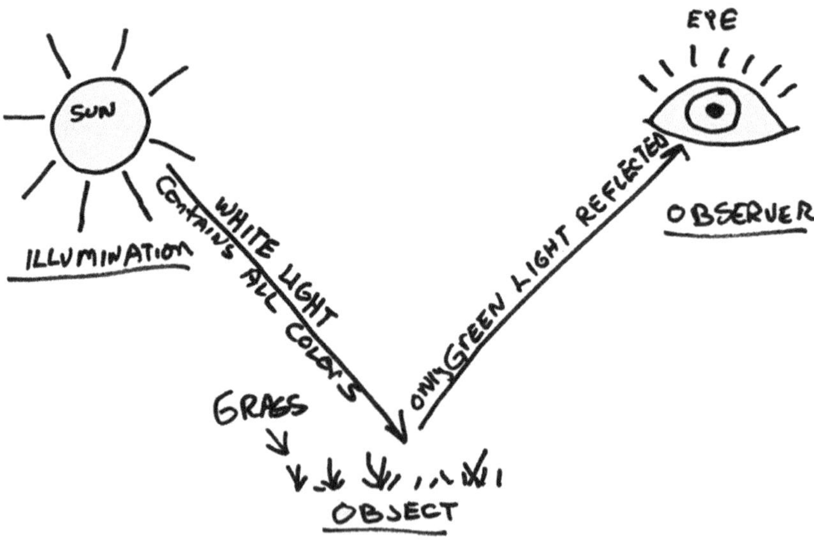

Figure 2. Eye, Grass and Sun

In this example, the sun will be our source of illumination. The sun is what we refer to as a white light source. What this means is that all of the various wavelengths of visible light, or colors are present in roughly equal amounts. This will make a little more sense in a moment, when we look at the electromagnetic spectrum in some detail. For the time being, just be aware that sunlight is made up of red, orange, yellow, green, blue, and violet wavelengths all in approximately equal amounts. Note that I didn't mention indigo. Yes, it's in the spectrum, but for the purposes of our discussion it's not really a significant distinction. The term "indigo" can be found in many older texts and describes color between blue and violet. It is also a term used to refer to a textile dye of vaguely that color, which adds another level of confusion. These days scientists don't consider indigo an important distinction and have dropped the term. It would be a bit like having a separate section on reddish-orange.

When all the different colors are present in roughly equal amounts, we perceive the color of the light to be white. We call this a white light source. You will notice that in Figure 2, the sunlight, which contains red, orange, yellow, green, blue and violet wavelengths is shining on a patch of green grass. The grass itself has no intrinsic color; however, it contains a pigment called chlorophyll, which soaks up the red, orange, yellow, blue and violet wavelengths just like a sponge. The green wavelengths, however, are reflected toward our eyes by the chlorophyll. Since only the green rays reach our eyes, all of the other colors having been absorbed, we perceive the grass as green.

As artists, we work with various types of pigments. Each of these pigments has the ability to absorb many and reflect one or more specific wavelengths of light. By mixing and applying different pigments, you can control which colors reach our eyes and which do not, therefore controlling the perceived colors. Pigments work in much the same way filters work with audio. They allow the artist to selectively add or remove certain wavelengths or frequencies to fine tune what the viewer ultimately sees.

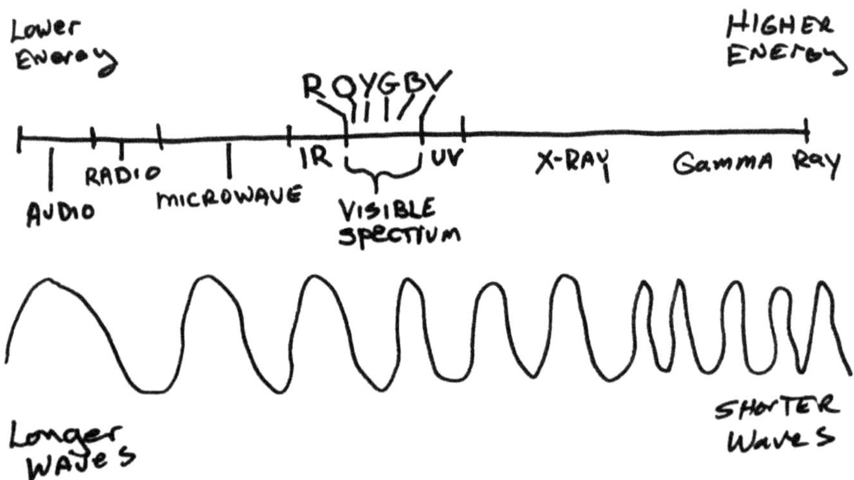

Figure 3 - The Electromagnetic Spectrum

Electromagnetic radiation consists of all of the different kinds of energy that vibrate or behave like waves. Visible light, of course, falls into this category, but there are many others as well. The electromagnetic spectrum is nothing more than a line, which we use to arrange all the various forms of electromagnetic radiation, in order of their wavelength. This line starts with the very long wavelengths of the radio waves, and at the other end, the very shortest wavelengths of the gamma rays. Right in the middle lie the wavelengths we are interested in the most, which we refer to as the visible spectrum.

The visible spectrum is just a tiny part of the electromagnetic spectrum (EMS), barely one octave in frequency (an octave represents a doubling of frequency). However, it's the only thing that matters to visual artists! Just like all the other waves in the EMS, the visible light waves are constantly vibrating at their particular frequency. The waves have peaks and troughs, and if you measure the distance between two adjacent peaks, you come up with a distance that we call wavelength.

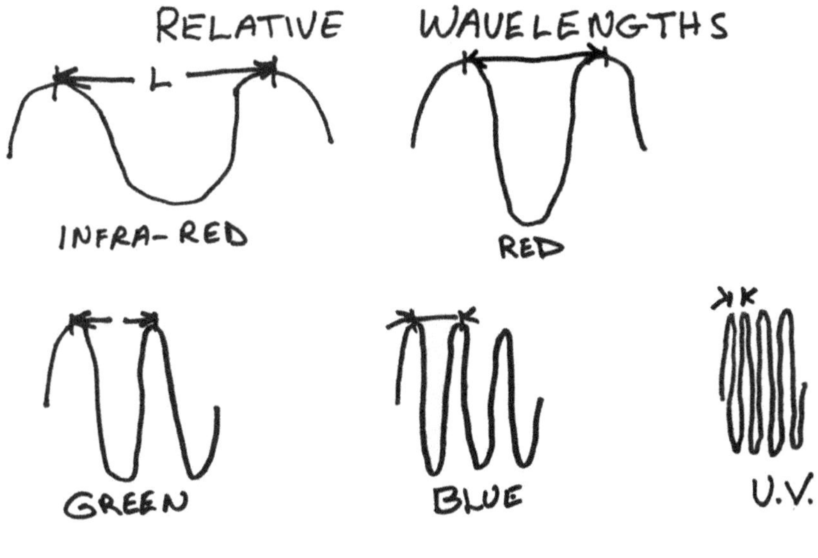

Figure 4 – Relative Wavelengths of Light

It is the difference between these wavelengths that allows us to differentiate between colors. You may have heard the term "warm and cool colors". At what we call the warm end of the spectrum, the waves are the longest, starting with red, then orange and yellow. As we move into the cool end of the spectrum, the waves get progressively shorter: green, blue, and the shortest, violet.

The eye is only able to detect wavelengths over a very narrow range, as I mentioned, about an octave. When the waves become longer than red, we call them infrared and even though we can no longer see them, we can detect them with our skin as heat. If you have ever been in a fast food restaurant and noticed those red lights that keep the fries warm for weeks at a time, you have seen an example of an infrared light at work. Even though the light warming the fries is invisible, since the spectrum is continuous, some of the red light leaks in and lends its distinctive color. When the waves get just a bit shorter than violet, we call them ultraviolet, which are the wavelengths that are responsible for suntan and sunburn. It is interesting to note that there is nothing inherently different about the ultraviolet or infrared waves that make them invisible, except their length. Just as some people can hear wavelengths beyond what we might call "normal hearing," some people can see farther into these bands than others. At some point though, everyone's ability to perceive these frequencies outside of the visible spectrum falls off very rapidly.

As a side note, there is a curious relationship between the ears and the eyes, with respect to how they handle wavelength and amplitude in opposite ways. Although the eyes can only see over a frequency range of about one octave (we call this color), they can adapt over a tremendous dynamic range in terms of amplitude (we call this brightness). You are able to see equally well in a candlelit room or darkened theater or outdoors in bright sunlight and still perceive subtle differences in brightness. In contrast, the ears are extremely sensitive to frequency (we call this pitch) and can sense very small changes over a range of about ten octaves. However, the ear is very insensitive to changes in amplitude (which we call loudness), and a sound must be considerably louder before we even notice a change.

At the back of the eye, there is a very sensitive area called the fovea, packed with photoreceptors, called cones. Each one of these types of cones is sensitive to one band or group of wavelengths. There is one type sensitive to red, one type sensitive to green and the third type, sensitive to blue. By varying the amount of each of the wavelengths that are stimulating the cones, we are able to perceive all the colors of the rainbow. I should mention at this point that there are more ways than one to cause the brain to perceive the same color. Take yellow for example. If we have a pigment which reflects a single wavelength just shorter than orange, but longer than green, (pure spectral yellow) we will see yellow. If we then try another pigment, which reflects equal amounts of red and green wavelengths, we will also perceive the same yellow color. This is a phenomenon known as metamerism (Fred W. Billmeyer, 1981), and these two examples would be called a metameric pair. In practical terms, this is why even though there is no pure magenta wavelength light in the spectrum, we perceive magenta when a color sample reflects equal amounts of red and blue light.

Spectral Content of Light

A prism, as Newton demonstrated, can be used to separate light into its component parts, because the different wavelengths are bent or refracted to different degrees as they pass through the prism. You can pass white light through a prism and out comes red, orange, yellow, green, blue and violet, all in order of wavelength. If you then feed these six bands into a converging lens, they will recombine to form white light again.

When a light source contains all or most of the different wavelengths of visible light, and these wavelengths are present in roughly equal amounts, we refer to this mix very broadly, as "white light." Sunlight, incandescent light, and fluorescent light are all examples of white light. Don't take this to mean that all white light sources will render color in the same way, this is just a very broad term for a light source that has many colors as spectral components (I must admit that the more I think about it, "white light source" is a terribly misleading and confusing term, but I'll leave that fight for another day or even another person). In fact, with some so-called white light sources used as streetlamps and in warehouses, the spectrum is so distorted that the light can cause sunburns, fade product packaging and cause trees and plants to become unhealthy. Some sources are so bad there was a need to come up with a scale called CRI or color rendering index, just so you could figure out how much your light source is distorting the way you see color. The CRI ranges from 0 to 100. 0 to 55 are considered poor at rendering color accurately and can have severe color distortions (there are even some with negative numbers, but they are rare). 60 to 85 are called good, but not for artists. 90 to 100 are more suitable for artists, galleries and museums.

As an artist or painter, the lights you use in your studio have a dramatic effect on the way your work will look in different environments. I use halogen spotlights or LEDs when I mix paint, but halogens getting harder to obtain. However, when I take my paintings out into the sun, or to a gallery, I am confident that the colors are correct. Always use a light source with the highest CRI you can afford if color is critical to your work. As a painter, I would only use lights with a CRI of 95 to 100.

Absorption and Reflection

Assuming no visual impairment, all the things that we see appear as images in our mind, because light has made its complex journey from the light source. The light sometimes being reflected off the surface of objects, sometimes being absorbed by other objects, then focused by the eye, translated into brightness and color information and transmitted along the optic nerve to the brain for further processing. When we look at a field of grass and it appears green to us. This is because the sun, which is a source of white light, illuminates the grass with all of the colors of the spectrum. The pigments in the grass absorb all of the colors except green, which is reflected. Since green is the only color reaching our eyes, we say the grass is green. If an object reflects all of the colors equally, all of the wavelengths reach our eyes, and we say the object is white. If all the light is absorbed by an object, no light reaches our eyes, and we say the object is black. I'll reiterate and elaborate on this important concept in the next section, but let it sink in for a moment.

CHROMA SUTRA

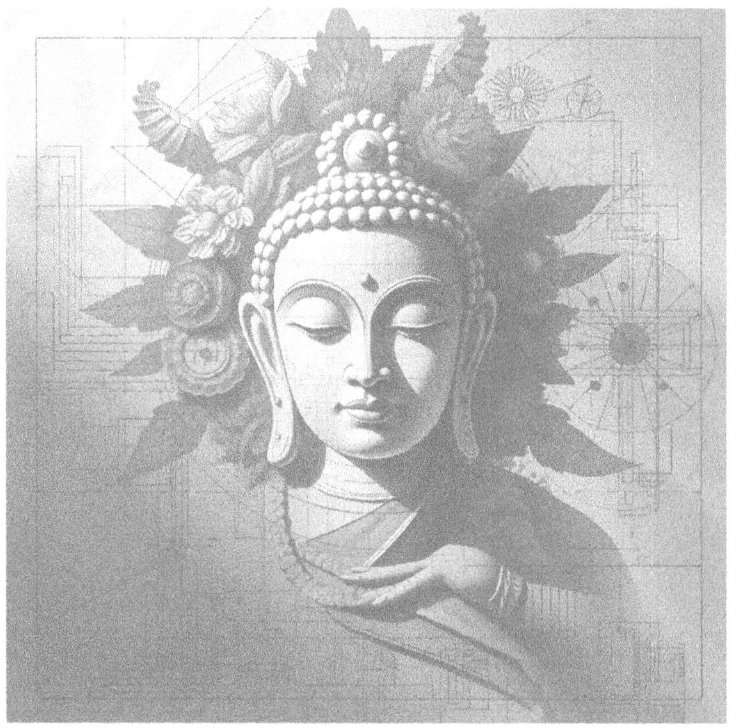

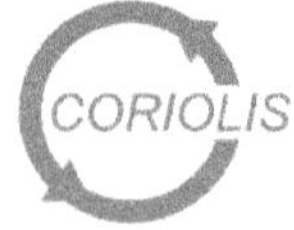

Chapter 3
Misperception of Color

Misperception of Color and Holland's Law of Reflection and Absorption

In addition to our eyes acting as measuring instruments, our brains constantly process the information relayed by our eyes, attempting to make sense of it. As it turns out, our brains are not very reliable instruments and are fooled quite easily. There are two rules which are very important to understand, concerning the way we perceive black and white. Understanding these two rules is crucial for an artist to have a solid grasp of color perception.

With all due modesty, I refer to this rule as Holland's Law of Reflection and Absorption. This law has two parts: The first part is that when an object reflects all the light that it is being illuminated with, we perceive it as white. The second part is that when an object absorbs all the light it is being illuminated with, we perceive it as black. These rules are true for the most part, without regard to the actual color of the object.

For example, in a totally black room, if we illuminate a red object and a white object with red light, they will both appear white. Since the red object reflects all the red light, and the white object also reflects red, (because it reflects all colors equally), both objects reflect all of the light they are being illuminated with. A more accurate description might be to say that they appear to be the same color, but since your brain has no real point of reference, you will conclude that they are white. In the same dark room, a blue object, illuminated with the same red light, will look black because it absorbs all the red light. Furthermore, consider this: under blue light, the same red object that looked white (under red light) will now look black (under blue light).

In many art courses, I regularly did a demonstration where I had a fluorescent red-orange card with a blue square in the middle. I would turn out the lights except for a red light on the card and ask the audience to identify the colors. After often heated discussion and debate (I believe they thought it was a trick question, which of course it was), the audience usually agreed that the squares were black and white. The students were always shocked to see the orange and blue when the lights were turned back on. So, one more time: since the orange reflected all of the red light, it appeared white. The blue absorbed all the red light, so it appeared black.

Let me give you one more experiment you can try to prove how easily white can fool your brain. You will need a piece of white paper, a notebook and a digital camera or a camera with daylight film. You can conduct a simple experiment to verify the accuracy of your perception, using the camera as a control. At three times during the day (just after sunrise, noon, and just before sunset) you should go outside and view the paper under the described lighting conditions. Write down the time, and the color that the paper looks to you. As a control, also take a photo of the piece of paper under the same lighting conditions and make notes so you can identify and match the photos to the notebook observations. For the fourth sample, view the paper at night under fluorescent light, and photograph that as well. As you might have guessed, the piece of white paper looked white under all four viewing conditions. But, when you develop the photos and match them to the observations, you find that the first and third photos are red, the fourth photo is green and only the second photo is white. What went wrong? Is there something the matter with the film? The answer is: no there is nothing wrong with the film, the paper changed color, and your brain didn't notice. The film cannot lie, all it does is record the wavelengths that are falling on it.

We need to go back to the concept of "white light" for the explanation. In all four examples our brain told us that the paper was white, because it reflected all of the light that it was being illuminated with. But this doesn't take in to account the actual spectrum of the source of illumination. Remember our old friend the CRI? The spectrum of sunlight is changing all day long and therefore the CRI is changing all day long. Some fluorescent light has a notoriously bad CRI (Free advice: It's not a good idea to apply makeup under uncorrected fluorescent light).

At times near sunrise and sunset, the sheet of paper is actually red. And there's a very good reason for that, which I'll tell you in a second. And under fluorescent light, the paper is green. But our brain is fooling us. I told you that any time something reflects all the light that it's being illuminated with, we say it's white. Well, it goes a little further than that. Whenever anything reflects all the light that it's being illuminated with, our brain tells us it's white, and we are convinced, regardless of what color it really is. That's one of the instances where our brain makes mistakes while it's trying to make sense of the world around us. Our perception of white light is quite unreliable. Photographers would say our "white balance" is changing constantly. And since we have no absolute point of reference, we say it's white.

Let's look at what white light means again. If I were to draw a little spectrogram here of white light, and we look at the components, they are red, orange, yellow, green, blue, and violet. This is what the drawings would look like. We have a simple chart with wavelength along the bottom axis from low to high frequency, and brightness along the vertical axis.

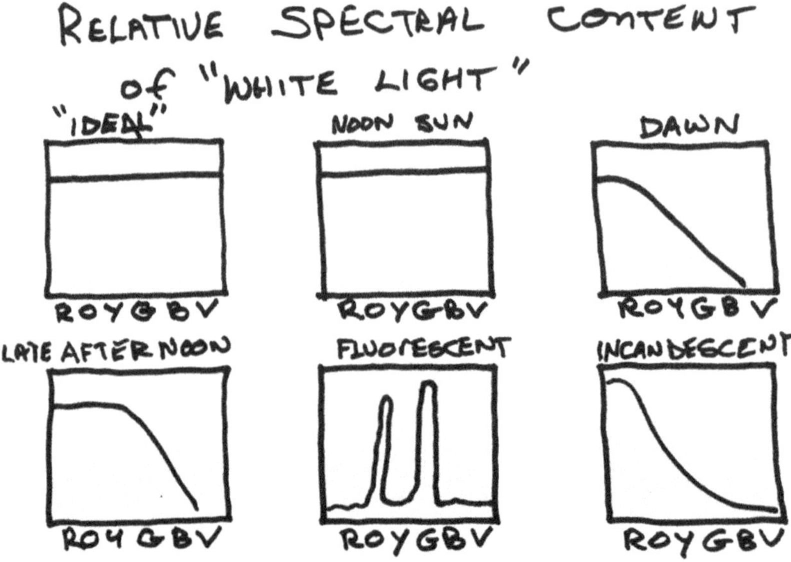

Figure 5 - Relative Spectral Content for White Light

White light, in theory, is supposed to contain equal amounts of every one of these colors, right? What happens at sunrise and sunset is that the sun is very low on the horizon and the earth's atmosphere blocks out a lot of the light. It just so happens that it blocks out almost all of the cool end of the spectrum. So, when the sun is low on the horizon, we're being illuminated with mostly red, orange, and yellow light. All of the green, blue and violet are attenuated.

That's why the paper is red in the first and third photographs. Because if you can picture it, the Gods are shining a red light on the paper. It would be just like taking a red floodlight and lighting it up with that. But our eyes fool us because since it reflects all the light we're illuminating it with, and we have no absolute point of reference. When an object reflects all the wavelengths of the illumination and signals that to the brain, it interprets the signal as though the object is white. Remember Holland's Law of Reflection. If we look at the spectrum of sunlight at noon, the spectral lines are almost perfectly even. So, when the paper is white, and you compare it to the photograph, it really is white. When I bring the sample paper to class with me, and we look at it under fluorescent lights, we have a different spectrum entirely. There is essentially no warm end of the spectrum. There's a huge peak right about blue and green. And then not too much violet. So, when we photograph it, the paper is very green. It is as though there was a bright green light shining on it. But your eye once again is fooling you.

The opposite rule which I call Holland's Law of Absorption also applies. Anytime something absorbs all the light that it's being illuminated with, we say it's black, regardless of what color it really is. If we take a blue piece of paper in a dark room, and we shine a red light on it, it will appear to be black. It will only prove to be blue when we turn back on the "white light" or full spectrum illumination.

Why is the spectral content of light so important? The spectrum of light gives us clues about the time of day, our environment, and even controls our Circadian rhythm. Let's take computer graphics as an example: first, understanding light and color and spectrum is extremely important. All the computer does is control the color of pixels at certain locations on the screen. Let's say you're trying to render a realistic office scene in an animated film. If you use the color spectrum for daylight, it's not going to look or feel like it's inside an office. It's going to look like it's outdoors somewhere. Or if you're trying to create a beach scene at sunset, and you use the color spectrum of fluorescent light, that isn't going to fly either. It's important to understand the differences in how light changes, how the spectral content changes, and how it affects the scene that you're trying to generate, whether it is on a computer or in a painting. I can't put enough emphasis on the importance of studio lighting that accurately renders colors if you are an artist or designer that specifies color in your work. If you paint by candlelight, your paintings won't look right when illuminated by museum lighting (Apologies to Goya).

Retinal Retention and Afterimage

I would like to spend just a moment on the concepts of retinal retention and afterimage.[1] There are several ways that the eyes retain information or get blasted into a condition that requires some recovery time. Sometimes we use the expression "letting our eyes adjust." If we walk from outdoors on a sunny day into a darkened movie theater it will seem pitch black until our eyes adjust. The eyes are always making adjustments for brightness and color correction, so the brain can make sense of the vast amount of information that we take in daily. Normally these changes occur gradually, and the eyes can take their time to adjust. However, when the change happens quickly, we can become disoriented or even temporarily blinded. Imagine you are in a dimly lit room, and someone flashes a flashbulb in your eyes. You won't be able to see for some time. One of the other curiosities of visual perception is that our retinas retain an image for about one-tenth of a second. This is the feature that allows us to see a television

---

1. We used to call it retinal retention, but now the thinking is that it may in fact, occur in the brain. This is the phenomena responsible for afterimage, flicker fusion and so on. This is the effect that allows television and movies to work, so we see motion instead of sequences of still images.

image that doesn't really exist, or to see smooth motion from still images on a movie screen. The other thing that happens is that when we stop looking at something, we often see an "afterimage." This concept of afterimage is an often-discussed basis for Itten's color work. When you stare at a red square on a piece of paper for a few minutes and then look at a blank sheet of paper, you will see a cyan square, which is of course the complementary color.

Primary Colors and Afterimage

I want to spend just a moment talking about afterimage, because I believe that this is where Itten made one of his biggest mistakes. This is something you can easily prove (I have included three examples below). If you stare at a bright blue square on a white piece of paper and then stare at a blank white piece of paper, you will see a yellow square. That is because blue and yellow are complementary colors, that is, they are opposite each other on the color wheel. The same is true for red and cyan, magenta and green and so on. I don't believe Itten fully understood these fundamental relationships or exactly what he was seeing, which led to much confusion in his books. Itten looked at green, and said he saw a red afterimage, although it would have been magenta. It may have even been a matter of semantics or translation error, but the information was ultimately found to be incorrect (I think his books are masterpieces and considered color bibles, and all artists should read them. Just don't take everything as gospel, as you would with any bible).

So why does this happen? Your eye is at rest with neutral gray. That is to say, when the three color receptors are being stimulated equally. Now, think of your eye as a pendulum. When you stare at one particular color, your eye swings to the maximum point of that color around the outside of the color wheel. When you then stare at a white sheet of paper, your eye swings to the opposite side of the color wheel, the complementary color, in an attempt to finally adjust to the mid-point of neutral gray. The swings will gradually decay to the point where you once again see the white blank paper.

Below, I have included three diagrams (figures 6, 7 and 8) that can be used to test your afterimage capability. These are similar to the tests that Itten would have performed in his experiments. The way they work is that you stare at the white cross on the color side of the diagram for about thirty seconds, then look at the black cross on the white side of the diagram and write down what color you see. I believe you will see the complementary color, which you can verify using any of the standard color wheels in this text. Let your eyes relax during the process. This is not a trick, it's just verifying the way your eyes are supposed to work, when they try to reach a natural equilibrium. Remember, that the natural state of the eye's relaxation is equivalent to neutral gray. After being exposed to one of the primary colors, the eye tries to regain equilibrium by swinging full tilt to the complementary color. In seconds, it will recover, and you will see the white page again.

This is a duplication of the experiments that Itten ran to determine the complements, and their placement on the color wheel. That is, ignoring the fact that he wrote down the wrong names for the colors he was seeing in the test, and then he started correcting things for the paint mixing results he was getting due to faulty pigments. All in all, not great scientific method.

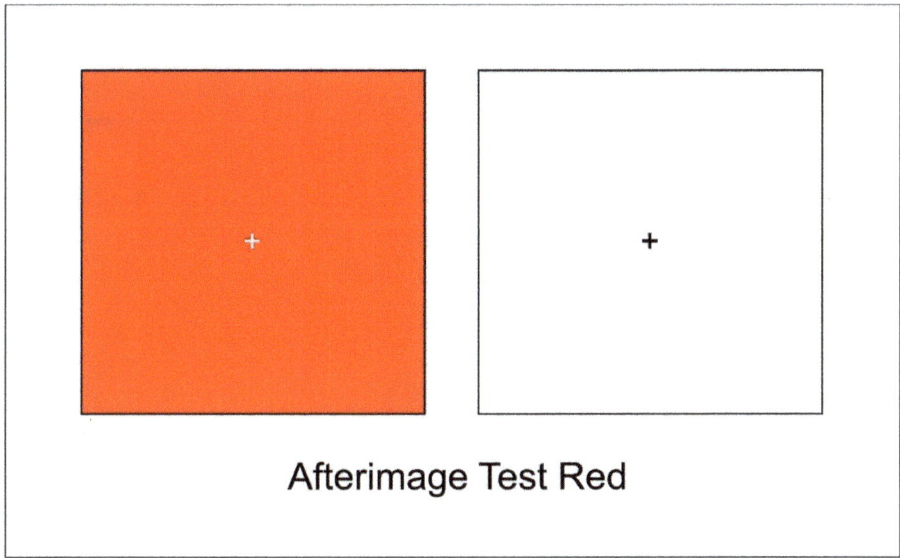

Figure 6 - Afterimage Test Red / Cyan

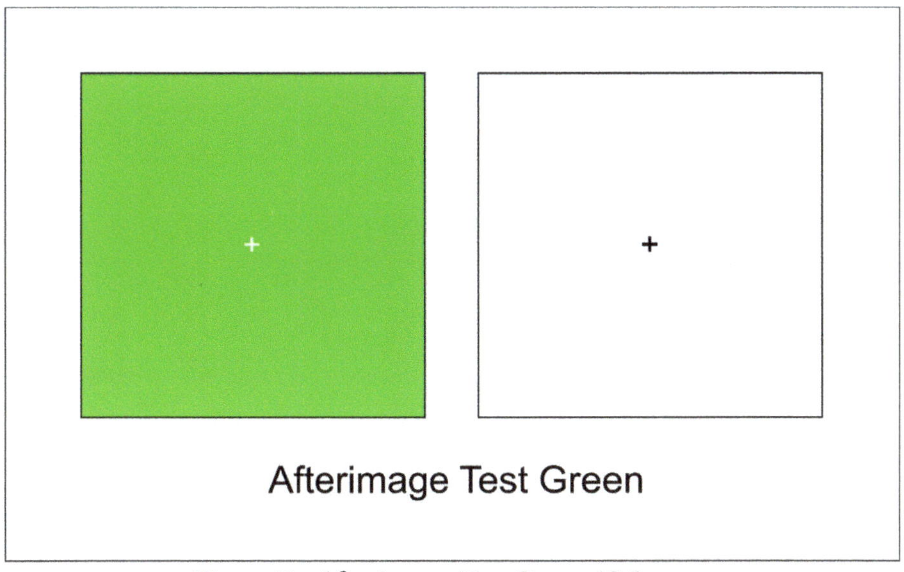

Figure 7 - Afterimage Test Green / Magenta

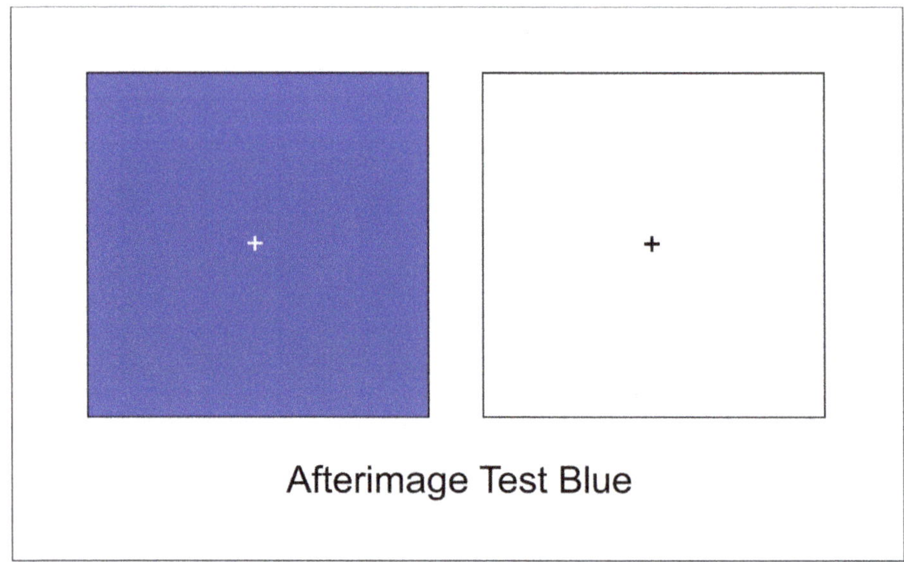

Figure 8 - Afterimage Test Blue / Yellow

Chapter 4
Systems of Color

Traditional Painter's Primary Colors

Almost inevitably, when I ask one of my classes to name the primary colors, the response is unanimous: red, yellow and blue. When I announce that this is incorrect, I am viewed with deep suspicion. As I explain that the primary colors are red, green and blue, I am faced with a sea of total disbelief. Quickly, it becomes evident from the looks on some of the students' faces that I have offended them, by assaulting one of their most sacred beliefs.

How did we get to this point? How could millions of students be taught the wrong primary colors? Who is responsible for this incredible misinformation, and how could such a ruse endure for nearly 300 years? It would be very difficult, (and perhaps unfair), to place the entire blame on one or two individuals. However, if we look back at the history of color, it becomes fairly evident just where this colossal problem began, and how, like urban legend, it was propagated.

In 1725, a French painter named Jacob Christoph Le Blon (Le Blon: 1667-1741) demonstrated that most colors of paint could be mixed from just three primary colors: red, yellow and blue. Even though this was not entirely correct, and Le Blon didn't have the high-quality pigments that we have available today, this was quite significant. One must consider that this was only about 30 years after Newton's discovery of the spectral components of light (Newton: 1643-1727). The next significant milestone came about 35 years after Le Blon, when an entomologist named Moses Harris (Harris: 1731-1785) produced the first two-dimensional color circle (what we now refer to as a color wheel), using the primaries of red, yellow and blue, and the secondaries of orange, green and violet. This is where progress with respect to color theory for artists stops. In fact, these are the very color wheels that an artist would purchase in any art store today and hopefully throw out after reading this book. Keep in mind that experts from all other technical fields know that your color wheels are incorrect. It's only artists who are taught the incorrect information and expected to use it.

The knowledge of color theory has been plowing ahead for 300 years, and yet painting students are still being taught that the primary colors are red, yellow and blue. I realize that I am beating this particular point into the ground, however, I feel that I cannot emphasize strongly enough what a huge scam this has been. Normally, and historically, students are very quick to point out any weaknesses or discrepancies in any material being pushed on them. Yet, I have never heard a student say: "Why is it that my photography teacher says that red, green and blue are the primary colors?" I have however, heard students ask: "If the color wheel is wrong, why do they keep printing them that way?" I must admit that I am a little embarrassed to answer that it is because that is what is being taught, and that is what sells. To paraphrase Ben Franklin: If misguided art students went not to market, bad color wheels would not be sold.

Determining the Primary Colors

Understanding now that red, yellow and blue are not the primary colors, the question that logically arises is: how do we determine what the primary colors are? How does a color become a primary color? It seems to me that one of the criteria for determining a primary color should be that it cannot be broken down into component colors. That is to say, it should be a fundamental building block of color. The second criterion, I believe, is that all other colors should be able to be produced by combining the three primary colors. The final deciding factor should be to look at the way our eyes perceive, differentiate and determine color.

On the back of the eye, in an area of the retina called the fovea, there is a high concentration of photoreceptors called cones. There are three different types of cones, each sensitive to different wavelengths of light, (or three different colors) that is, Red, Green and Blue. It seems logical that if the entire spectrum of colors we see can be perceived using sensors that respond only to three different colors of light, that all colors can be produced using only three colors of light. It should then follow further that we should be able to reproduce all colors, using only three colors of pigment. If these pigments are carefully chosen to precisely stimulate the three receptors in the eye, they should automatically meet the other two criteria previously established for determining primary colors.

The complication that now arises is that we see colors by combining different wavelengths of reflected light, and that combination is an additive process. Mixing pigments, however, is a subtractive process, as we will explore in the next section. Therefore, when using pigments, we will have to complement our primary colors to account for this phenomenon.

In order to understand clearly the idea of additive and subtractive color systems, and the fact that red, green and blue are the primary colors, let's revert for a moment to the system of color that most people were taught, and already understand. I will refer to this system as "Painter's Colors" and from here, we will quickly pass over this primitive idea so we can begin refining our understanding of additive and subtractive color systems. Imagine a diagram of three overlapping circles, with the painter's primaries of red, yellow and blue filling the non-overlapping portions of the circles. In the overlapping portions, red and yellow combine to make orange, blue and yellow combine to make green, and blue and red combine to make violet. If we mix equal portions of red, yellow and blue, we generally produce some form of brown!

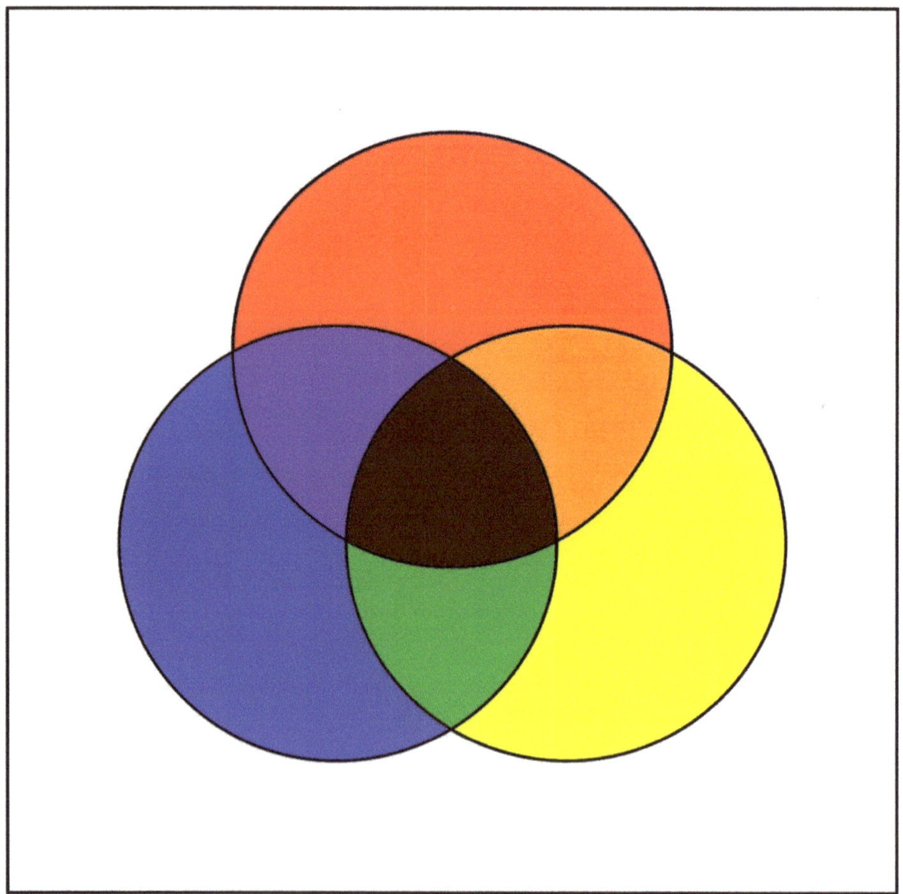

Figure 9 - Diagram of Painter's Primary Colors

What's Wrong with this Picture?

It is extremely important to keep in mind that this painter's color wheel, the one that is almost exclusively used to teach art students, now and for the past 300 years, is simply incorrect! The major problem with this historical color wheel is that it doesn't contain magenta or cyan. Neither of these colors can be made by mixing other colors, and both are required to accurately mix the remaining colors. This color wheel has been adjusted to compensate for the way that pigments, particularly inferior pigments, misbehave. As an example, theory will tell you that mixing yellow and blue should make black. However, with cheap pigments, or pigments that are not of the precisely correct hues, mixing yellow and blue will almost certainly yield green!

The answer historically has been to just change the color wheel to indicate that yellow and blue make green. I can assure you, however, that using pigments of sufficient quality, and choosing the proper hues, yellow and blue will always combine to form black! In addition, adjusting the color wheel to match the performance of poor pigments creates serious problems down the line. Besides confusing the hapless students of color theory, it also means that now the rules of perception are behaving differently than the rules of mixing paints. In essence, the theory of mixing colors begins to diverge from the theory of perceiving colors. This divergence or dichotomy creates a huge and frustrating problem for artists and is the reason I spent my career searching for the grand unification theory of color.

One of the theories of color design and composition states that the eye is like a scale, and that when all of the primary colors are present in combination, which represent equal amounts of each, the eye will be in proper balance, and the effect will be pleasant and harmonious. In other words, if you have a painting that contains equal amounts of red and cyan, which are complementary, the eye and brain will perceive neutral gray, therefore being in perfect balance. While this is true, this is a critical point of failure for the theories of colorists like Itten and others. The theory points to the fact that red and cyan are complementary; however, when they mixed their inferior pigments, the only way they were able to obtain gray was to mix green and red. Because the early colorists' experiments were poorly constructed, and their pigments were of poor quality, faulty results were obtained. Based on these results, they modified their philosophical and hypothetical conclusions to match the erroneous experimental results. Itten even went so far as to convince himself that after staring at an image of red pigment, he would see a green afterimage. Give it a try, and I believe you will see a cyan afterimage.[1] The paint mixers, like Itten, are teaching you that the eye wants to see orange and blue together to be in balance and harmony, even though the perception teachers know our eyes require yellow and blue to be in balance. They have postulated an incorrect perceptual theory, from poorly controlled practical experiments. The early professors of color have "corrected" their color wheels to be incorrect!

One additional matter that further complicates the accurate discussion of color is the fact that the names we apply to colors tend to be very technically imprecise. I will go as far as to say that no color name, other than those that refer to groups of wavelengths, or measurable quantities

---

1. You can repeat Itten's experiment by using Figure 6 in this book. In fact I have supplied images to repeat all three of Itten's after-image tests.

such as Hue, Saturation and Value, have any real worth to the student of color.

You need only pay a visit to the local paint store to see excellent examples of this phenomenon. In just one aisle, I was able to locate the colors of "Moondance," "Cherub" and "Vapor." I cannot begin to imagine what is inside the opaque cans! Even names like "Navy Blue" or "Kelly Green" leave tremendous latitude for interpretation.

The color red for example, can span from violet to orange, with dramatic differences from one end of the range to the other. And the description of red tells me nothing about the saturation or value. One person's green might be nearly blue while another's might be reaching towards yellow. As we now take a closer look at the subtractive primaries, we will begin to refine both the actual hues of the primary colors and the names by which we will refer to them. Hue, Saturation and Value are the most important qualities which we will use to describe colors. This is called the HSV system, and you may also see the RGB system which is used for light and the CMYK system which is used for printing.

What are The Primary Colors? What are Additive and Subtractive Primary Colors?

Now that you have a diagram of the painter's primaries, we will begin to hone this idea a bit and produce what are referred to as the subtractive primaries. This is the color wheel used to represent subtractive processes, like mixing pigments and colorants, and of course, artists' paint mixing. Mixing paint is called a subtractive process, because each pigment only reflects a very small portion of the light that it is illuminated with. The light that is reflected determines the color that we perceive. The rest of the light is absorbed like a sponge and never reaches our eyes. Because each pigment absorbs most of the total light that would be reflected, each time we mix two pigments together, there is much less light reaching our eyes. We have in essence created a new color, by subtracting out all of the colors we are not interested in. When you mix two colors of paint together, the resulting color is always darker than the two colors you started with; unless of course you add white! The reason for this is that if you mix blue and red for example, the blue pigment subtracts out all of the colors in the spectrum except blue. The red pigment subtracts out all of the colors except red. This only leaves a very small amount of red and blue light available to be reflected toward the eyes, where they combine to make violet / magenta.

This process of subtracting wavelengths of light leaves us with an interesting semantic problem. As painters, when we think we are adding cyan to a color, what we are in fact doing is subtracting red! When we seem to be adding yellow to a color, we are actually subtracting blue. As we add magenta to a color, we are in actuality subtracting green. Since it is fairly difficult for most of us to think in these inverted or complementary terms, we solve the problem by complementing the colors in the additive primary system and calling it the subtractive system.

One can only imagine the confusion that would arise, if painters spoke in the additive color parlance: "I believe what is lacking in this mix is a little minus red." Can you envision Vincent writing to his brother: "Theo, please send me two tubes of minus green, and a tube of minus blue," when what he really wanted was magenta and yellow? As absurd as this sounds, photographers and people who use filters in their work routinely think in these negative terms. Once we look at both the additive and subtractive systems in more detail, this will make a lot more sense, and you will see that they contain the same information.

I can't tell you how many times I have heard a student say "Oh, but that only works for mixing light," or "Let's see you mix white paint from all the colors." These statements show a complete lack of understanding of the underlying principles of color. Please keep in mind that the additive and subtractive systems are identical. They each contain exactly the same information, and either one can be used to solve problems in either the additive or subtractive domains. The only reason to choose one system over the other is to compensate for the semantic inversion inherent in switching between domains and to prevent the struggling artist from having to speak in negatives.

In the additive domain, mixing all colors will yield white, or neutral gray at the highest value, because we have overwhelmed our eyes, by adding together all of the colors of light. In the subtractive domain, mixing all colors will yield black, or neutral gray at the lowest value, because we have starved our eyes for light by subtracting all of the colors of reflected light. All other information regarding color behavior remains the same, albeit inverted with respect to the complementary system.

The Subtractive Primaries

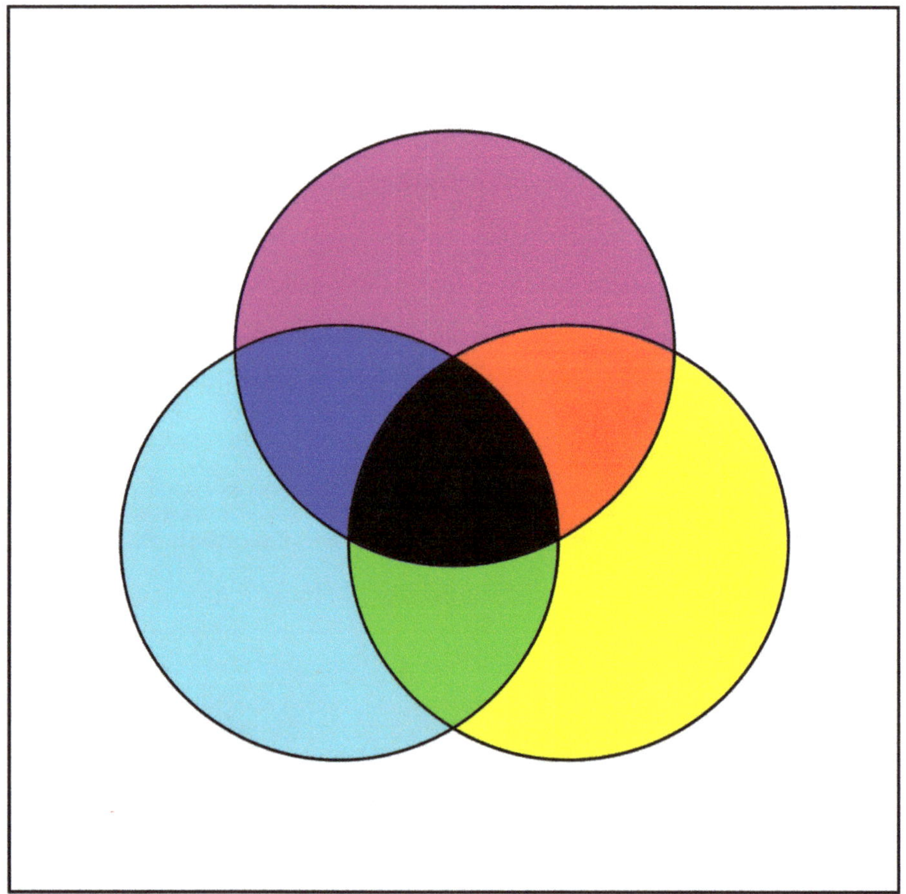

Figure 10 - Diagram of Subtractive Primary Colors

We have already drawn and familiarized ourselves with the diagram we called "Painter's Primary Colors." Now we will use the same diagram (Figure 9) but we will adjust the colors slightly, to make the relationships between them more accurate. Beginning with the top circle, instead of filling it with red, we will select a color just slightly to the left on the color wheel, (the counterclockwise direction), called magenta. Magenta is the very first color in the red group that lies nearest to violet. Magenta can be thought of as a color that is found exactly halfway between red and violet. In reality, there is no magenta wavelength in the visible spectrum, but we perceive magenta as a separate color when our eyes are stimulated equally with red and blue light. In order to make a color wheel, we take a linear spectrum, ranging from the long wavelengths of red, to the short wavelengths of violet, and we bend it around in a circle. Where the two ends of the spectrum meet, they form magenta. As we move clockwise to the next circle, we will select primary yellow. This is a very pure, bright yellow that painters will be familiar with as cadmium lemon. For the final color, instead of blue, let's make a correction slightly counterclockwise, to a color called cyan. Cyan sits exactly halfway between blue and green on the color wheel, and painters will be familiar with it as thalo blue-green.

Holland's Law of Primary Complements

One interesting note is that each of these colors seems to be sharing or bordering on two other colors. Because of the way our vision works, a pigment can either reflect a pure wavelength such as yellow, or it can reflect a pair of primaries such as red and green. In either case, we will perceive the result as yellow. It is fair to think of the subtractive primaries as reflecting a pair of additive primaries, and absorbing the third additive primary, which would be its complement. This is called Holland's Law of Primary Complements, which states that the complement of any primary color is the sum of the other two primaries. This concept forms a very valuable rule for painters: given the three primaries of magenta, cyan and yellow, if you want to know what the complement of any one of them is, simply mix the other two. For example, if you were using magenta, the complement would be cyan plus yellow, which yields green. Green is in fact the complement of magenta. Now that we have examined the painter's primaries and corrected them to form the more accurate subtractive primaries, let's take the idea one step forward to form the additive primaries.

The Additive Primaries

The additive primaries are merely the complemented version of the subtractive primaries, and we use them when we are talking about mixing light. We will start with the same diagram as the subtractive colors, utilizing three overlapping circles. In the top circle we will place the additive primary of red. In the second circle, we will place the additive primary of green, and third will get filled with the additive primary of blue. Where the red and blue circles intersect, we will place magenta, which is formed by the combination of red and blue light. At the intersection at the bottom of the diagram, we place cyan, which is formed by the combination of blue and green light. In the remaining intersection, red and green combine to form yellow light. In the center, red, green and blue combine to form white light.

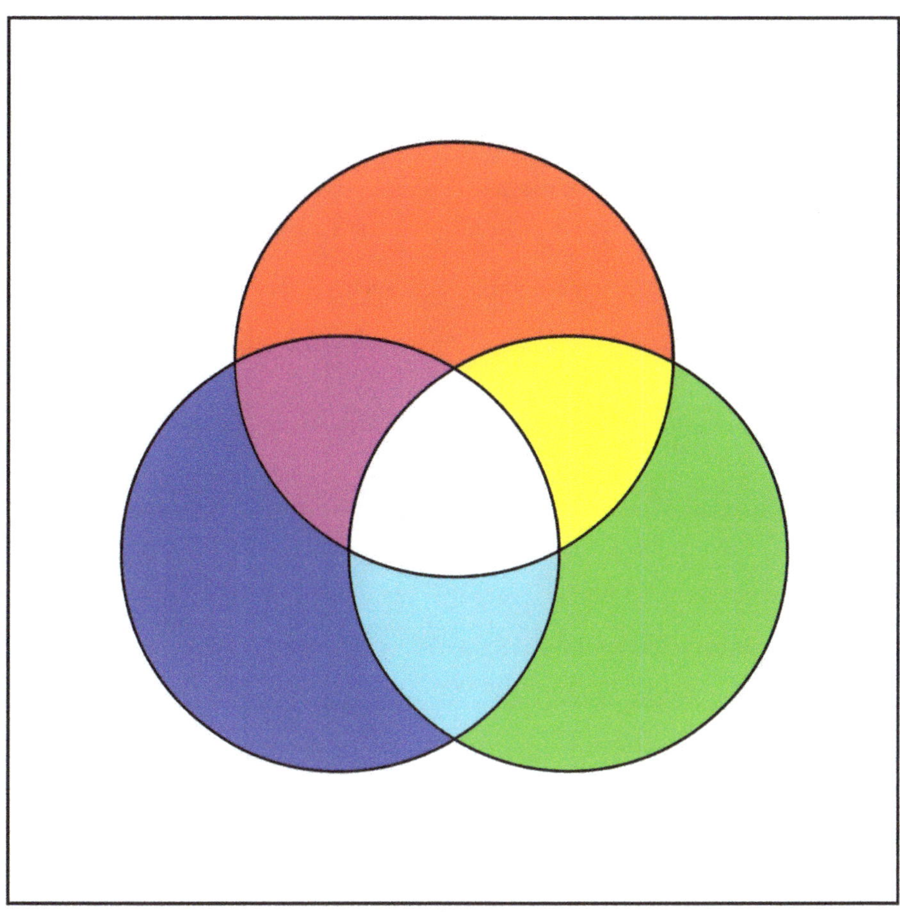

Figure 11 - Diagram of Additive Primary Colors

I realize that as painters, this new diagram will seem very foreign to you, but these are in fact the primary colors, and this diagram shows how the eye perceives color. Before you throw your hands up in disbelief and disgust, let's look a little more closely at the additive and subtractive diagrams side by side. The first thing you will notice is that the primary colors in the subtractive diagram have become the secondary colors in the additive diagram, and vice versa. Just for the moment, we will define the complementary color as the color directly across from our key color on the color wheel. We will refine this definition a little later in the book. If you draw a line directly across from red in the subtractive diagram, you will find that the complement is cyan. If you draw a line directly across from red in the additive diagram, you will find that the complement is also cyan. If you try any of the other complementary combinations, you will find that they indeed are the same in both diagrams. All of the information contained in the two diagrams is exactly the same! Any color problem can be solved with either diagram. The only reason that we have two versions is to compensate for the matter of semantics, so we don't have to talk about yellow as minus blue.

Let's look at two of the other differences that become obvious. You will notice that in the subtractive model, any time you combine two colors, the resulting color is darker than the two you started with. As you recall, that is because you are creating a new color, by subtracting out all of the colors you are not interested in. You are starting with white light and subtracting everything except the color that results from your mix, and ultimately reaches your eyes. In the additive model, any time you combine two colors of light, the resulting color is lighter than the two you started with. That is because you are creating a new color, by adding two colors of light, to arrive at the new resulting color you are interested in. The new color causes twice as much light to reach your eyes as either one of the colors you started with.

The final difference is that in the subtractive model, all three primaries combine to form black, which is neutral gray at its lowest value. Any time you have equal amounts of the three primaries, in either system, neutral gray is formed. Neutral gray just means that the resulting color is equidistant from the three primaries and does not tend towards any of the primaries. That is to say, if a painter mixes neutral gray, it should not have a yellow tint, a cyan tint, or a magenta tint and so on. The reason black is formed in the subtractive system is that by mixing all three primaries, you have subtracted out all of the colors of reflected light, so no light reaches the eyes. When no reflected light reaches the eyes, we perceive an object to be black. Remember Holland's Law of Reflection and Absorption. In the additive system however, when all three primary colors of light are mixed in equal amounts, white is formed. White is also a form of neutral gray, but at its lightest value. By combining red, green and blue light, all of the cones in the eye are stimulated maximally, and we perceive this mix to be white.

One other small side note: When you were taught the erroneous painter's primary colors, you were also taught that when you mix two primaries together, the result is called a secondary color. There are also tertiary colors that result from mixing secondaries with primaries. I don't generally spend much time talking about secondary or tertiary colors. I don't find the concept to be very helpful or enlightening. As a foundation, the concept of primary colors is essential to understanding color. However, from that point on, all other colors are the result of mixing two or three primary colors in various proportions. In fact, as you study the additive and subtractive color systems, you will find that when you mix equal amounts of two primaries together, the result is not so much a secondary color, but a primary color in the complementary system. So, while the concept of secondary colors is not incorrect, as you become more aware of how color systems work, you will just find that the concept is not very useful.

Another thing that should be obvious by now is that on the painter's color wheel that you were exposed to in school, you learned that red and blue were primary colors. We now know that red is made by mixing magenta and yellow, and blue is made by mixing cyan and magenta. Red and blue are only primaries in the additive system, and we don't use the additive system for mixing paint! I don't even want to get into red and green being opposite on "painter's color wheels." Are you starting to see the problems?

Putting it All Together

I would like to propose that we build an accurate color wheel, consisting of 12 colors, placed on a circle, so that each color is spaced 30 degrees from its neighbor. This will be a sort of composite color wheel, which contains both the additive and subtractive primaries, and can be used to solve most color problems. We will start with a large circle and divide it up like a pie with 12 slices. The reason that we use the number 12 is because that is the number of basic colors that are necessary to accurately represent harmonic relationships. However, an equally important reason is that an artist can easily visualize and remember 12 distinct colors, without much effort. We could just as easily use 24 or 144, but if we were to use many more colors than 12 for our basic set, visualizing them becomes a much greater chore.

The other important goal we will achieve with this composite color wheel, is to come up with a naming convention that works in both the additive and subtractive domains and eliminates the ambiguity of imprecise color naming. I did not come up with this concept, but it doesn't seem to have a standard name, (and as I have said, most available color wheels are inaccurate) So I'm going to suggest we call this the "Holland Standard Composite Color Wheel for Artists."

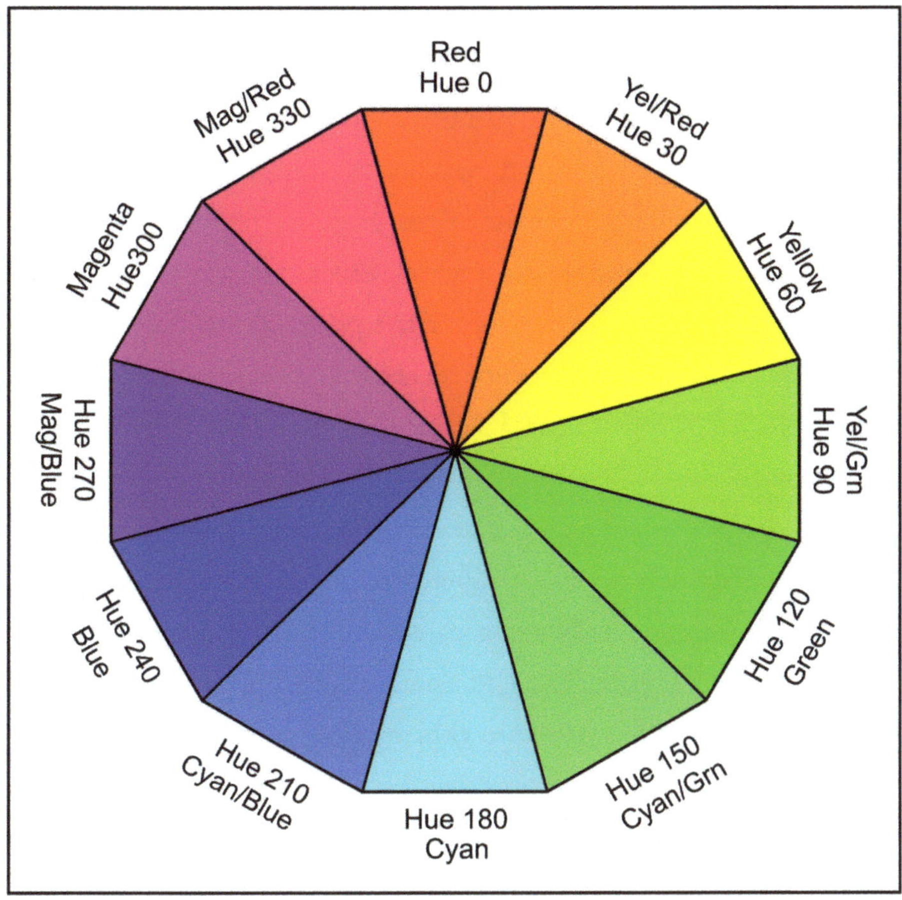

Figure 12 - Diagram of Holland Composite Color Wheel

We will start at the top with the additive primary color called red. Painters will be familiar with this color as cadmium red medium, a sort of fire engine red. Red is always placed at the top of the composite color wheel, according to convention. In fact, all of the hues around the outside of the wheel have standard numbers associated with them. Red is hue 0 (or 360 for the purposes some calculations). The rest of the numbers count around the circle clockwise, until they meet again at red. Each position number matches its position in degrees around the circle. At the position of 120 degrees, we place the color we will call green. Primary green is very intense, and perhaps a bit yellower than what one is used to calling green. As it turns out, the eye is more sensitive to green than any other color. Continuing around the wheel to the 240-degree position, we place the color blue. The color we are looking for is what painters call prussian blue. It is a very deep blue, halfway between cyan and magenta. At this point, we should have filled in the three additive primaries of red, green and blue, and they should be spaced equally around the color wheel, 120 degrees apart.

The next step is to place the subtractive primaries into their positions on the wheel. Directly across from red, at the 180-degree position, we will place a color called cyan. Cyan is a color that is exactly halfway between blue and green. Painters will be familiar with it as thalo blue green (sometimes written as phthalo or even phthalocyanine). At the 60-degree position, we will put primary yellow, which painters will recognize as cadmium lemon, a very bright pure and usually transparent yellow. Next, at the 300-degree position, we will insert magenta. Magenta is a color halfway between blue and red, which painters often see as being close to madder lake, alizarin crimson and so on.

The spaces that remain will get filled with colors that are made by mixing the two colors on either side of the blank space. This particular placement of colors is based on a mathematical precision that will allow a considerably more predictable color mixing scheme and will make the understanding of harmonic relationships much easier for the student, as we will see in later chapters. The color that goes in the 30-degree position is called red yellow. It lies halfway between red and yellow and is the color we normally think of as orange. We will, however, refer to the color as red yellow for reasons of precision. Likewise, all of the rest of the colors that we will fill in will be referred to as combinations of the names of their two color neighbors.

As a general convention when we name colors, we just start at the top of the wheel and name them all in the same order around the wheel. Since each of the combination colors is made up of equal amounts of its two neighbors, the exact order of the names isn't critical. However, for the sake of neatness we generally name them in the same order. When naming the tertiary colors, we generally use the protocol of primary-secondary. In the first example yellow is the primary and red is the secondary. So, if we call the first combination yellow red, the second one would be called yellow-green, followed by cyan green, and so on. In a 12-step wheel, yellow green is the same color as green yellow. However, it is important to note that if there were more positions than 12, say 24, this would no longer be true.

Now that we have completed our precise, composite color wheel, you may have noticed some striking differences between this wheel, and the one that most artists were taught in school. You will probably notice that instead of having green directly across from red, you find cyan across from red. Instead of showing violet as the complement of yellow, we find blue. And instead of the familiar orange and blue being complements, we find that the true complement of the color we used to call orange is actually cyan blue. All these changes were part of the process of correcting the traditional color wheel. These are also the reasons that most painters find color mixing to be a struggle. This is the explanation for all of the muddy colors on your palette, and the fact that you ended up with brown far more often than black. Prepare yourself for a burden to be lifted, and a true feeling of liberation as we start experimenting with color mixing using our new subtractive primary colors.

CHROMA SUTRA

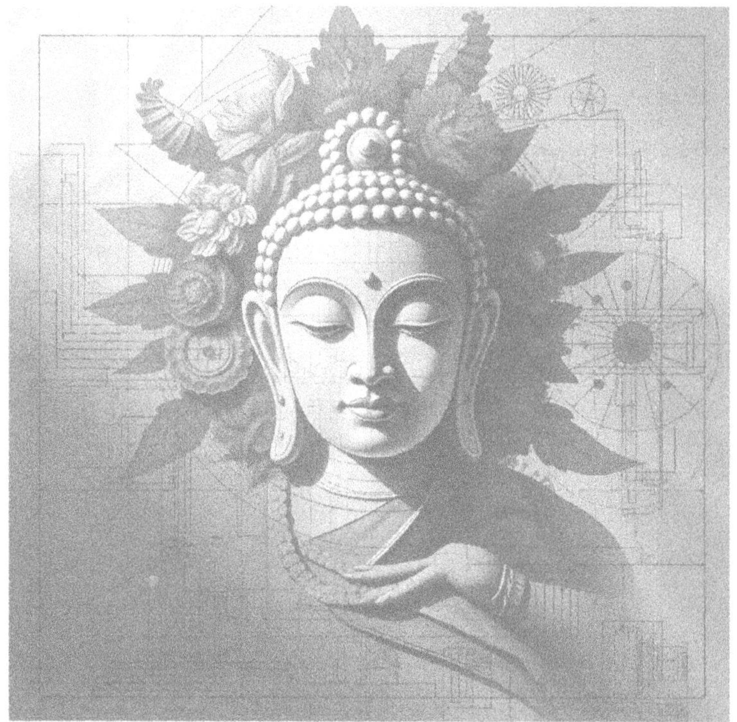

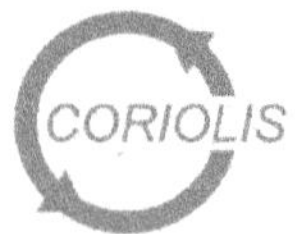

Chapter 5
A Tri-Color Approach

Primary and Secondary Colors

In this section, I will show you how to dramatically simplify your color mixing by using a tri-color palette. I will teach you a new way to look at color as a painter. I will also give you some exercises to greatly enhance your color perception skills. We will be working with only 3 colors, the subtractive primaries of magenta, cyan and yellow. We will also use white so we can create the class of colors known as tints. I would recommend using Maimeri Classico Oils, because of the enhanced ability to get the correct results. I'm not a paid spokesperson. It will make your job of learning color mixing much simpler, and then you can graduate to any oil paint brand you like. For this palette, I would choose Titanium White, Magenta, Primary Yellow and Thalo Blue Green.[1] Keep in mind we are using the thalo blue green as cyan, so in the future I will usually refer to it as cyan, except when I forget and call it thalo. Squeeze a bit of the primary colors out onto your palette, and we will begin mixing colors. As you mix the colors, you could

---

1. These are the Maimeri Classico paint numbers that I am recommending for these excercises: Magenta (256), Thalo Blue-Green (410), Primary Yellow (116) and Titanium White (018).

print out the blank color wheel from the back of this book or draw your own. As you mix the colors, place them on the color wheel at the proper hue number location. When you are finished, you will have a permanent reference you can hang on your studio wall next to your easel. I will also add that the more time and precision you put into making your color wheel, the more useful it will be in the future.

At this juncture, I would like to introduce a concept known as "tinting strength." Tinting strength is the ability of a pigment or colorant to impose its color on the mixture. Another way of looking at it is how strong the pigment is compared to the other components. In an ideal world we would say: mix one part white with one part cyan, to get a color halfway in between, but that won't really work because the cyan packs one serious amount of tinting strength. If you want to arrive at a mixture that looks halfway between white and cyan, you may need ten parts white to one part cyan. You will pick this up very quickly, and it's always better to ease into your color mixes (by adding small amounts of paint) when you are starting out. Therefore, if I say mix a color halfway between thalo blue green and white, I mean visually, not by volume. For these experiments, the thalo blue green is the strongest, magenta is next and yellow is by far the weakest. Just keep this idea of tinting strength in mind as you work through these exercises. As you get better and better at mixing, you will be adjusting for tinting strength constantly, however it will be essentially automatic.

Let's start with a little bit of yellow. If we add to that a little bit of magenta (keeping in mind that the magenta is much stronger than the yellow in tinting strength) we can get a color that matches cadmium red. I know, you thought red was a primary color, but we just made it with magenta and yellow. So much for the American education system. But I digress...Your red should appear exactly halfway between magenta and yellow. That is to say it should not be too orange, or too violet; it should be cadmium red! That is how you will know you have it.

Now let's again start with yellow and add a tiny touch of thalo blue green. The goal is to have a color called primary green, sort of a Kelly green. You don't want it to be either too blue or too yellow, but exactly halfway in between.

Now we will mix blue. Start with a small dab of magenta and add a tiny bit of thalo blue green. The result you're aiming for will be like prussian blue, familiar to painters. Once again not too blue green and not too violet. Right in the middle, (once again, I know you thought blue was a primary color, but here we are).

Building a Color Wheel

We have started with our three subtractive primary colors; magenta, cyan and yellow. We have also mixed three secondary colors; red, green and blue. Notice that the secondary colors in the subtractive system are the primary colors in the additive system? You should always remember that the information in both systems is the same; we complement the colors when we work with light instead of paint. Not to beat it to death, but if we were doing theater lighting or color darkroom printing, we would use the additive system. We would start with red, green and blue light as primaries. The secondary colors that we create by mixing primaries would be magenta, cyan and yellow.

When we have mixed these six main colors, which we call the primaries and the secondaries, we can place them on the color wheel at their hue locations sixty degrees apart. But what colors go between these colors? They are called tertiary colors. You will see that starting at the top of the color wheel, we have red, (hue 0) then a space, then yellow (hue 60) and then a space.

Let's start with hue 30, a color that we call yellow red. In the old days you may have called it orange, but we're way past that now. So, to make yellow red, we take some of the red we mixed, and slowly add a bit of yellow until it is halfway between red and yellow. (It will look orange.) Eventually, your painter's eye will develop to the point where you can get it exactly in the middle of the two colors. Plop it down on your color wheel.

Now let's make hue 90, a color that we call yellow green. In order to make yellow green, we take some of the green we made and slowly add a bit of yellow until it is halfway between green and yellow. When I say halfway between, I mean visually, measured with your eyes. It should fall exactly between the two colors. Not closer to yellow, and not closer to green. Once it is perfect, add it to your color wheel.

Next mix hue 150, a color that we call cyan green. In order to make cyan green, we take some of the green we made and slowly add a bit of cyan until it is halfway between green and cyan. It should be exactly in the middle of the two colors. Add it to your color wheel. (Keep in mind we are using the thalo blue green as cyan, so I will refer to it as cyan. I will elaborate on this in the section on the Holland Ten Color Palette).

Now mix hue 210, a color that we call cyan blue. In order to make cyan blue, we take some of the blue we made and slowly add a bit of cyan until it is halfway between cyan and blue. It should be exactly in the middle of the two colors. Add it to your color wheel.

Next make hue 270, a color that we call magenta blue. In order to make magenta blue, we take some of the blue we made and slowly add a bit of magenta until it is halfway between magenta and blue. It should be exactly halfway between the two colors. Add it to your color wheel.

Finally, let's make hue 330, a color that we call magenta-red. To make magenta-red, we take some of the red we made, and slowly add a bit of magenta until it is halfway between magenta and red. It should be exactly halfway between the two colors. Place it on your color wheel.

So, to recap, we started with three primary colors: cyan, magenta and yellow. Using those three colors we mixed nine more colors to fill out our twelve position color wheel. Now congratulate yourself on the success of step one, and we'll move on to some more advanced colors.

The Basics of Three-Color Mixing

I realize that most artists are not accustomed to mixing with three primary colors, especially when they are not the three that you learned were primaries. However, I think you will adapt very quickly. One process that I believe you will find helpful is to constantly ask yourself the following questions: Is my mix too magenta, too cyan or too yellow? If the answer is too magenta, add green (yellow and cyan). Too cyan? Add red (yellow and magenta). Too yellow, add blue (magenta and cyan). Sometimes an artist has 50 tubes of paint in his box and will use five tubes to mix one color. This makes it almost impossible to know how you got there, and even harder to duplicate. When you are using only the three primary colors, it is so much easier to see what a mixture needs. Do I need to add magenta, cyan or yellow? Perhaps two of those? Once you become good at mixing with only three colors, the task becomes very easy, very repeatable and considerably less wasteful. Once you get really good at this, go back to doing anything you like with your 50 tubes. After all, you have learned a powerful new skill, and now you can bend the rules. In fact, the only rule in art is that there are no rules.

In this first diagram (Figure 13), I show the basics of three-color or tri-color mixing using the subtractive primary colors of cyan, magenta and yellow. In the top row, we have the three primaries right out of the tube. In the second row, we mix magenta and yellow to make red. We mix magenta and cyan to make blue and then cyan and yellow to make green. It also shows how we make black by mixing cyan, magenta and yellow. After we mix the black, we can add white to make an entire range of neutral grays. This is also a good way to test your black mixture to be sure it doesn't tend towards any of the primary colors (that is too yellow, too cyan or too magenta). I also take the red we made and create a few tints, tones and shades by adding white, gray and black respectively.

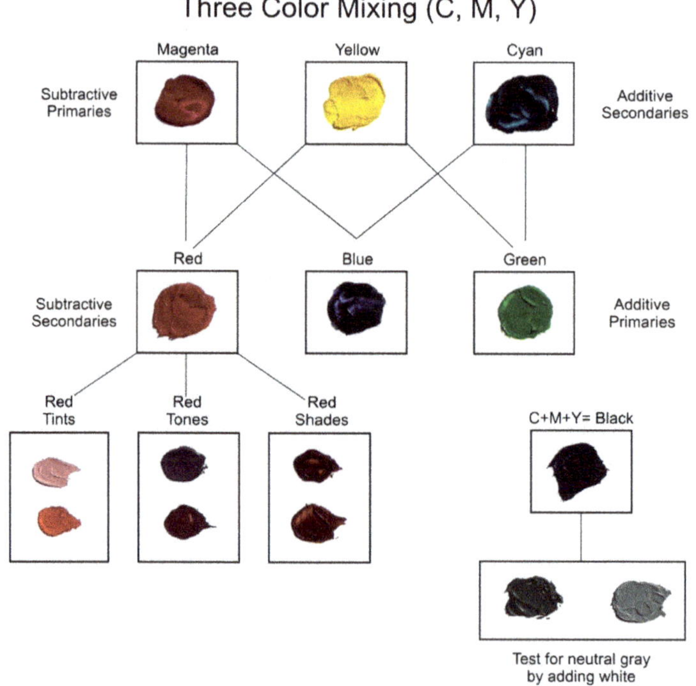

Figure 13 - The Basics of Tri-Color Mixing Using CMY

In the next diagram, I hand mix a complete reference color wheel using the three primary colors. In the widest ring I have the pure hues, starting with red at the top (remember red is always hue 0. You can look at some of the other color wheels in this book that have the hue numbers added). In the outer ring I have mixed a bit of white with each of the pure hues to produce tints. For the thin grayish ring in the center, I have added gray to the pure hues to make tones. The ring nearest the center has black added to the pure hues to make shades. On the right, I made some black and added white to create a neutral gray chart of values. I would encourage you to make yourself a chart like this to practice, and I have included a blank form in the reference section of the book for you to copy. When you have finished, you will find it very useful to keep next to your easel as a constant reference for harmonic relationships. Keep in mind you already threw out the one you bought at the art supply store.

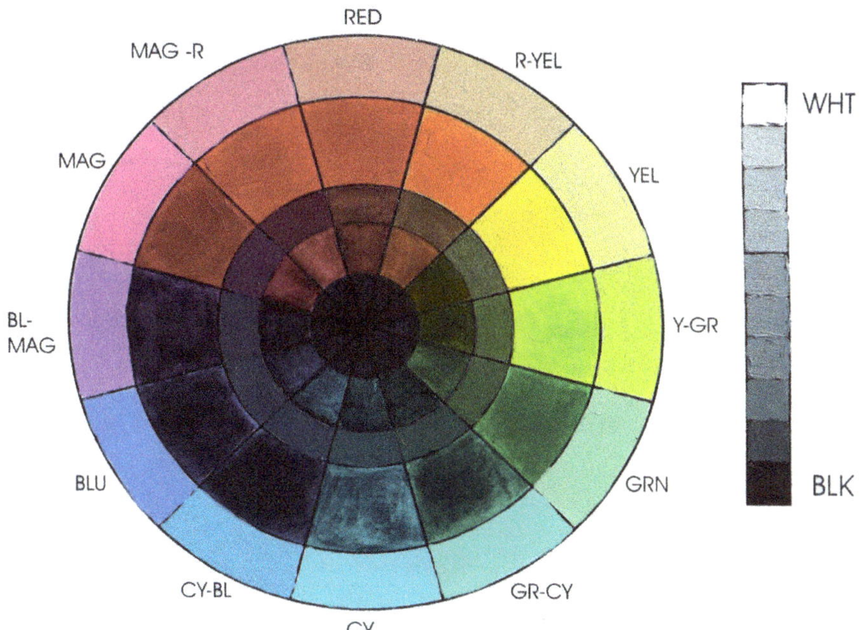

Figure 14 - Three Color Mixing CMY With Tints, Tones and Shades. (Using Maimeri Classico)

In the next section, I demonstrate some of the families of color mixing possibilities using the three color approach. I have broken the charts down into four families, the reds, greens, blues and earths. Of course, there are many more, but this will give you some inspiration to start mixing on your own.

Whenever I begin this discussion, I think of the poor student who has 10 different tubes of green in his paint box, yet none of them is ever the precise color he needs, and none of them look realistic in the lighting scheme of his painting! This problem is more common than one might imagine, and exceedingly easy to solve. Let's start with the greens, for example, and give it a try: We make green by adding varying amounts of cyan and yellow. I don't have any greens in my everyday paint box, since if I can describe it, I can mix it.

If we look at the middle row, the first three are just yellow, with increasing amounts of cyan added. The last two also have a touch of magenta added to make them more realistic or more like the colors you would expect to find in nature. In the upper row, I have added a bit of white to make a tint. In the lower row, I have added a bit of black to make a shade.

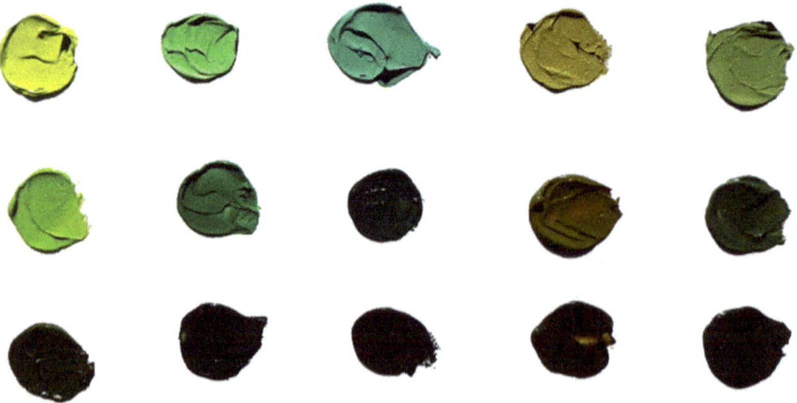

Figure 15 - 3 Color Mixing Cyan/ Yellow Series

In the next set we mix up some of the warm end of the spectrum from magenta to yellow. Once again, we look at the middle row. In the first position, we have pure magenta, and in the last position, we have pure yellow. In between, we start with magenta and increasingly add yellow. None of these mixes use cyan, just to show the array of colors you can make with just two tubes. In the top row, I add white to make tints. In the bottom row, I add black to make shades.

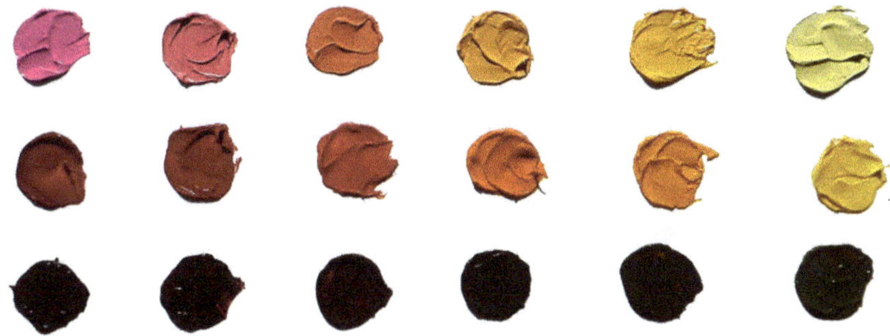

Figure 16 - 3 Color Mixing Magenta / Yellow Series

In the next set we mix up some of the cool end of the spectrum from cyan to violet. Once again, we look at the middle row. In the second position, we have pure cyan, and in the first position, we have added just a touch of yellow. For the rest, we start with cyan and increasingly add magenta. In the top row, I add white to make tints. In the bottom row, I add black to make shades. I also cheated just a bit...the shades were almost black, so to make them easier to see, I added just a touch of white also, which technically makes them tones, not shades any longer.

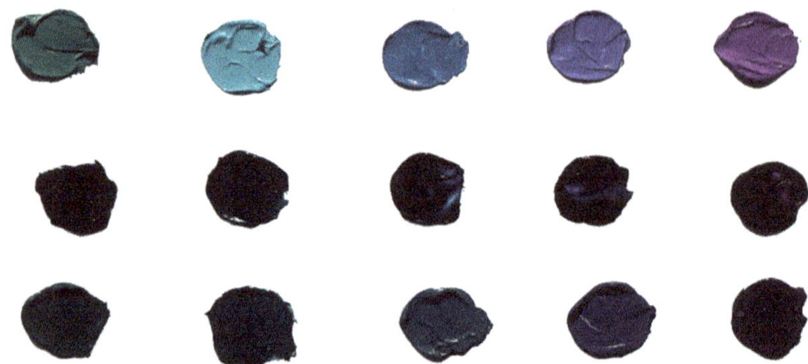

Figure 17 - 3 Color Mixing Cyan / Magenta Series

Now we'll mix up some of the colors we normally refer to as Earth Colors. They are called that because most of them are made from pigments mined from the earth. Sometimes they are washed or raw, sometimes roasted, sometimes even burnt. Still just dirt though. That would be the ochres, umbers, siennas and oxides, to name a few. All of these colors are simulated from differing proportions of all three primaries. Once again, we look at the middle row. In the first position, we have magenta mixed with tiny bit of yellow and a tiny bit of cyan. In the last position, we have started with magenta and added almost equal amounts of yellow and cyan. In between, we start with magenta and increasingly add yellow with a touch of cyan. You may notice that the more yellow you add, the more ochre like it becomes. The more magenta you add, the more it looks like the red earths and the siennas. In the top row, I add white to make tints. In the bottom row, I add black to make shades.

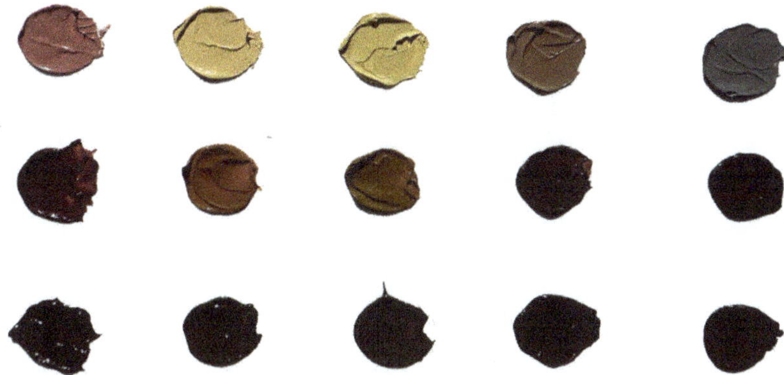

Figure 18 - 3 Color Mixing Series Earth Series

CHROMA SUTRA

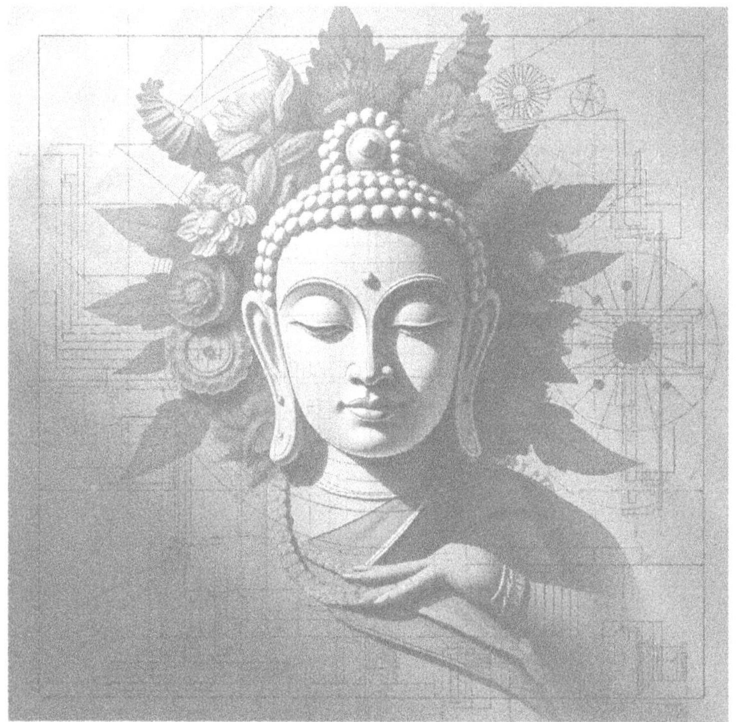

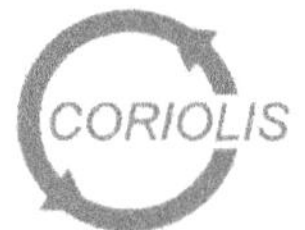

Chapter 6
Exploring Color Space

Describing Locations in Color Space

Color Space is a term that refers to the limits of the gamut of colors that you are constrained to in your work. Let me give you some examples: If you are given two tubes of paint, you will be limited in the number of colors you can create by mixing the two colors. You will be limited by the practical resolution of the way you measure the amounts of paint you mix together. That is, you can't take five cubic centimeters of one color and add three molecules of the other. You might be able to mix 10 parts of the first color, and one part of the second...or maybe you will mix three parts to one part of the second. But you can see how there are practical limits to the number of different colors you can mix with those two. So, if we take the totality of the number of colors we can make with the two tubes of paint, let's say we can make 500 different colors, this is called the gamut of our color system. It means all of the possible colors that can be created or reproduced within a given set of constraints or limitations.

What about your eye's ability to discriminate color? That depends on many factors like age, color training and ability to describe or verbalize the differences. Believe it or not, some people recognize less than 20 different colors. If you ask them what color the sky is they will reply blue. Ask them what color denim is, the answer is blue. These are two very different colors, yet some people lack the interest, or the ability to discriminate, or simply have never thought about it. Perhaps they lack the vocabulary to describe differences in color even though they can perceive them. The trained colorist has the ability to differentiate somewhere between 8 million and 17 million colors. Yes, 17 million! That means a trained colorist might be able to distinguish between a million different shades of blue! Unless you are colorblind or have another perceptual barrier, most people can be trained to perceive many more colors than they do currently. As an artist, you very likely are more sensitive to color than most and already perceive dramatically more colors.

All color systems have what is called a gamut. That is to say, colors that can be reproduced within that system. Any colors that cannot be reproduced are said to be outside the gamut. Now that we understand the limitations of gamut, we need to think about how to represent the concept of color space itself. There are many ways to represent color space, in both two and three dimensional models. I have seen flat, two dimensional color wheels, color cubes, color spheres and very elaborate organically shaped multi-dimensional models. In industrial applications where the science of color is extremely advanced, some of the color models are also equally advanced. However, as an artist or painter something much simpler like a color cylinder will teach you everything you need to know to be a master colorist.

A Simple Exercise for Building Color Discrimination

I'm going to give you a simple exercise that is both fun and challenging. Go to your local house paint store and peruse the color samples. They're free so take as many as you like. I would suggest you get at least 20 different cards covering all major hues. You could take 100, but I guess let your conscience be your guide. If you feel guilty, just buy some art supplies you need anyway. Like maybe, paint thinner?

Now pick one of the cards and set yourself up with the three primary colors and white oil paint. Make sure you have a good, bright, high CRI light source. Your challenge is to pick one color on the card and try to match it exactly. You should be able to mix the color with such precision, you could paint it over a corner of the sample, and you can't see a difference. Will you get it perfect the first time? Maybe, but not very likely. If you must, do it two or three times. Keep at it until you nail it! Keep asking yourself, is it too magenta, too cyan or too yellow? Is it too light or too dark? Once you have matched the color exactly, pick another card and repeat the whole process. This is not a very long exercise. (Although it wouldn't hurt to repeat it once in a while, to keep in top shape). I would suggest that if you do this with maybe five different colors, in different hue families, you will have already improved your color discrimination dramatically. You may notice this in other areas of your life, in addition to just art. For example, on a long drive you may start to look at the passing foliage and see 10,000 shades of green instead of the 10 you are used to seeing. This is like a workout at the gym for your color perception. I think you will be amazed at the progress.

Hue, Saturation and Value

One might ask, why do we need three dimensions to describe a color? One of the best and most accurate ways to describe a color is to use a color model like hue, saturation and value. If you are using a computer, you might see this as hue, saturation and lightness but it works the same way. Let's look at what these three terms mean, and how they allow the artist to convey in great detail the technical description of a particular color. Let's begin with hue. Hue can be thought of as a family of colors, or a specific pitch of color. Reds are lower pitch; blues are higher pitch. Hue is nothing more than a location, or where the color falls on the circumference of the color wheel. We say that yellow is a different hue than green. If we want to get even more technical, we can assign a hue number to the location on the color wheel. As an international standard, red is always at the top and is assigned hue 0 (or 360 for some calculations). Cyan is at the bottom and is hue 180. So, with just the first term, hue, we have a way of describing 359 different colors and their precise location on the color wheel. Artists typically use a color wheel divided into 12 sections, so each of the hues is 30 degrees apart. This makes it easier to visualize and remember.

Now let's move to the term saturation. Saturation refers to the amount of pure color that exists in a sample. Imagine a scale where at one end you have neutral gray, and at the other end you have the pure color. I'll use red as an example. If I start with a very bright, intense red, I can think of that as maximum saturation. That is the reddest it can ever be. Now slowly start mixing in a neutral gray. The result is you are reducing the saturation and getting closer to a brick red. Eventually, you will add enough gray that the color no longer has any red in it at all and is just gray. We call this minimum saturation because we can no longer determine hue. Red at minimum saturation is gray, so is blue at minimum saturation, and so is yellow. At zero saturation, we can no longer determine the hue of any color sample.

The third and last parameter that we need to describe a color completely is called value (or lightness). Now imagine a scale that runs from white at the top, to black at the bottom. One can compare the color sample to that scale. It is easy to imagine a light pastel blue somewhere near the white end of the scale, whereas a dark navy blue would fall near the bottom of the scale, closer to black.

By using these three qualities of hue, saturation and value, we can very accurately describe any color on our palette. We can even describe the colors to another artist or manufacturer so they will know precisely what color we want them to reproduce. We can say we want blue at hue 240, with a saturation of 35% and a value of 72%.

Building Our Three-dimensional Color Space Model

Now jump back to the idea of a three-dimensional color space. Imagine your two-dimensional color wheel with the hues at 100% saturation around the outer edge. As you move towards the center of the circle, the saturation is gradually reduced so that when you reach the center of the circle the saturation is 0%. The center of the wheel will be gray, and the colors will become brighter and more saturated at the outer edges. With only two dimensions, you have represented hue and saturation. Now how do we represent value? This is why we need a three-dimensional model to represent our color space. Imagine now that your color wheel becomes a color cylinder. We could slice this cylinder into 100 slabs like a stack of pancakes. Each circular slice could represent that same hue and saturation information, except with the value term added. The slice at the very top of the stack would be completely white, since hue and saturation data are meaningless at 100% Value. The slice in the very middle of the stack would look like your normal color wheel, because the value is 50%. The slice on the very bottom of the stack would be pure black since hue and saturation are meaningless at 0% Value. All colors become black! We have created a three-dimensional model where all colors can be located in the color space. Every color that exists can be found somewhere in our stack of colors. Every color from red to violet, no matter how bright or dull, no matter how light or dark.

Tints, Tones and Shades

I would like to spend a couple of minutes talking about tints, tones and shades. These are terms you hear every day, but few people realize they have very specific technical meanings. A tint is when you take a particular hue and add white. Imagine a scale where you have white at the top and a color at the bottom. Let's use red as an example. At the bottom you have fire engine red, and at the top of the scale is white. Light pastel pink is very near the top. Light red might be somewhere in the middle. As you start at the bottom, you have a pure color, and as you move up you are adding more and more white. These are called tints.

A tone is where you are adding gray to the color. Sometimes artists refer to this as graying down a color mix. Imagine the scale now has a pure color at the top, and neutral gray at the bottom. We start with a pure color, and by adding progressively more gray we move down the scale. At the top, our fire engine red starts to become brick red as we add gray, when we get near the bottom, it becomes more of a reddish gray.

Finally, we get to the term shade. You often hear people say "that's a nice shade of blue" but they could be referring to anything. Technically however, shade means a color with black added. Imagine this time, we have a scale with our pure color at the top and black at the bottom. Let's say we have bright blue at the top of our scale, as we start to add black, it becomes progressively darker and moves towards navy blue, and then on to black. These are the colors one sees in the shadows...and thus, shades.

Chapter 7
Color Harmonies and Relationships

Primaries, Secondaries and Tertiaries

In order to understand color harmonies and the relationships of one color to another, we need to understand the terminology used to describe classes of colors. We have extensively covered the primary colors, used in both additive and subtractive color systems. Since artists use paint and pigments (pigments can include inks, dyes and powders) for their work, it is understood that we will be using the subtractive primaries for this discussion of harmonies. We are referring to the primary colors as magenta, yellow and cyan. Note that the additive and subtractive theories contain exactly the same information. As a result, this section can be used for either theory, if one remembers to complement the color data.

So, if the primary colors are magenta, yellow and cyan, we know we can also create a set of what we call "secondary colors" by mixing any two primary colors. If we mix magenta and yellow, the result is red. If we mix magenta and cyan, the result is blue. If we mix cyan and yellow, the result is green. One thing you will remember is that the secondary colors in the subtractive system are the primary colors in the additive system. This may seem like black magic but remember both systems use the same data. Just remember to use the subtractive system for paint mixing, and the additive system for light mixing (such as computer monitors or theater lighting).

If we mix magenta, yellow and cyan, the result will be black. In fact, by mixing different proportions of the three primary colors, we can create any color possible. However, for now, let's just confine the discussion to simple mixtures of two colors at a time.

We know that we have three primary colors: magenta, yellow and cyan. We now also have a group of three secondary colors: red, green and blue. So, let's create a group of "tertiary colors" by mixing a primary color and a secondary color. I believe you know my opinion of "color names," so I will discuss a preferred way of referring to colors we mix.

If we mix red with magenta, we get a color called magenta red. This would be located on the color wheel halfway between magenta and red. When we construct a color wheel, the simplest one just has six positions: The primary colors, and the secondary colors. The primaries are separated by 120 degrees, and the secondaries are located between the primaries. You can look at any secondary color and know that it is created by mixing the two primaries on either side of it. If we want to include tertiary colors on the wheel, we generally divide the wheel into 12 equal parts, (30-degree sections) and put the tertiaries next to the colors used to mix them. When naming the tertiary colors, we start with the primary color used, then a slash mark or space, then the secondary color used. So, in the example above, we mixed magenta, the primary color and red, a secondary color to make magenta red...halfway between magenta and red.

You can see by extension, we could make six tertiary colors called yellow red, yellow green, cyan green, cyan blue, magenta blue and magenta red. As you can see, these names are very descriptive. They tell you exactly where the colors are on the color wheel, and which colors were mixed to create them. If you always list them in this order, you also know magenta red has more magenta and some yellow. You can easily visualize the precise colors. This is one reason we normally limit the color wheel to 12 positions. Most artists can easily visualize the exact colors and interpolate the rest. Any more than 12 would start to be unnecessarily cumbersome. This color naming convention is very descriptive and technically precise. In addition, you can start to see the nonsense in calling a paint color "whispering wind".

Just to go one step more towards the technical, all the colors on the color wheel have what we call a "hue number." That's what we use to describe precisely where a color falls on the wheel. Red is at the top, and that is hue 0. Cyan is at the bottom, and that is hue 180. All the other primaries, secondaries and tertiaries are 30 degrees apart. So as an example, yellow/red is hue 30, yellow is hue 60. Green is hue 120. Magenta is hue 300, all the way back to red which is 360 or 0. Red is almost always referred to as Hue 0, but sometimes when doing calculations, it can be known as hue 360. Not critically important, one knows one is back at the beginning. The hue numbers just go clockwise from red to red 360 degrees, in 30-degree steps. Now, of course, in industrial applications, we might describe colors in even more precise ways[1] , but for artists, this level of description will suffice. If you would like to investigate industrial color further, a good starting point would be here: (Fred W. Billmeyer, 1981).

---

1. In the world of industry, there are many complex ways of cataloguing and matching color: The Munsell System, Pantone Matching System, RAL Color System, The CIE System and many others. These are necessities for industry, but not really required for the work of most painters.

If you would like to follow along with these examples using your computer, please see the chapter on "Using a Computer to Study Color" for some helpful suggestions.

Complementary Colors and Complementary Hues

The terms complementary colors and complementary hues are often used as though they were interchangeable; however they are very different things! Complementary hues, which are almost always what we are referring to in discussions of color harmony, are nothing more that colors that are opposite each other on the color wheel. Any two hues that are 180 degrees apart on the color wheel are said to be complementary hues. If you know that one of your hues is yellow (hue 60) and you want to know its complementary hue, just add 180 degrees (or look at the opposite side of the color wheel) and you will see that blue (hue 240) is the complementary hue. Why do we call these hues complementary? Is it because they go well together? Well, yes and no. Technically when you put complementary hues beside each other, they create a maximum contrast of hues, which can be visually jarring. But when you physically mix any two complementary hues, the result will be black. So, if you mix yellow and blue, you get black. Mix red and cyan, you get black. Mix magenta and green, you get black. Any two complementary hues make black! One should keep in mind that a statement such as this is theoretical and ignores the quality of the paint. With good paint, the theory and practice are the same, and this will be true. With cheap paint, all bets are off with regard to results.

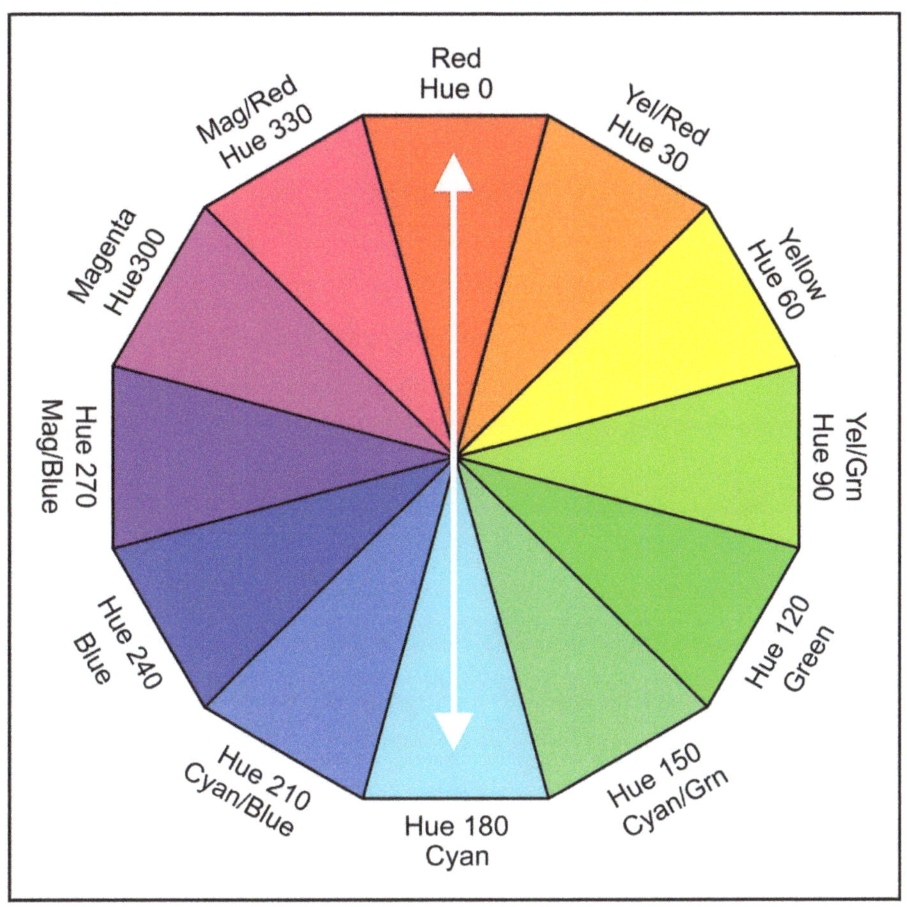

Figure 19 - Diagram of Complementary Hues

Now, let's get back to the difference between complementary hues and complementary colors, and why there is a difference between the concepts. It has to do with color perception, and the way the eye and visual perception system works. The eye is a sensitive, delicate measuring instrument. Whenever it is stimulated with equal amounts of red, green and blue light, (think about the light reflecting off of your pigments) it registers as a neutral gray color. With lots of equal RGB light the eye perceives white. When there is no RGB light, it perceives black. With a medium amount of equal RGB light, it sees neutral gray. And neutral gray is the state that the visual and perceptual system feels comfortable with. The eyes like to return to equilibrium, that is neutral gray. If you stare at a red dot, on a white piece of paper, then look at a plain white piece of paper, you will see a cyan dot. Those colors are 180 degrees apart on the color wheel. By staring at a red dot, you made the pendulum of your eye swing to 0 degrees (hue angle). By looking at a white page your eye/brain perception system swings 180 out of phase, trying desperately to reach equilibrium again. If you stare at the page long enough, your eye will once again become balanced and you will see white, that is all receptors receiving equal stimulation.

When we talk about complementary hues, we are referring to hues that make our eyes (and our entire visual perception system) slam back and forth from maximum to complementary maximum, 180 degrees apart. This explains the visual hyperactivity we experience when we place complementary hues in close proximity to one another in a painting. We use complementary hues when we are talking about color theory and the color wheel.

Now let's talk about practical applications. If we want to design a color scheme that is pleasing to the eye using complementary colors, we need to consider other aspects of color like saturation and value. This is where the concept of complementary colors becomes handy. The definition of complementary colors is two colors that when combined form a neutral gray. We know that combining cyan and red will result in black. But what if your main color is a slightly dark cyan (so it has a brightness about 30% less than white, and full saturation). We know that the complementary color would be a lighter red, with full brightness and saturation about 30% down from full red.

To understand this concept more easily, we look at the HSB (hue, saturation and brightness) model of color on a computer. Use any art program that lets you edit color, using models such as RGB or HSB. Let's type in our cyan as H=180, S=100 and B=70. What do these numbers mean? Well, the first part tells us that the hue is 180, which we know is cyan. The saturation is 100% so we set S to 100. This means we don't want any gray. We want the brightness to be 30% down from white which is 100, so we set brightness to 70. This results in a slightly darker cyan.

We can calculate the complementary color easily: We know that we want the complementary hue, so we set H=0. (Complement = (H+/-180)). Saturation and brightness of the complementary pair just get swapped, so saturation is now 70% and brightness is now 100%. This makes perfect sense since our cyan was slightly dark, we know the complementary red must be slightly light.

Let's solve this problem one more way using the RGB model. This method may be easier for people who are not overly familiar with using the computer. Since we are using an additive model (RGB), the maximum is always white. The numbers are always listed in order of R then G then B. Numerical values range from 0 to 255. A value of 25 for red means: the red is only 10% above black. A value of 255 for red means the red is full blast (or as red as it gets).

So back to our example pair of complementary colors. The cyan, slightly dark, would be entered as 0/179/179. We know cyan is made from equal amounts of green and blue (in the additive system) so this makes sense. We also know that we want the cyan at 70% brightness, so we enter the two components, green and blue as 179 (179 is 70% of 255).

So how do we figure out our complementary color from the RGB values? Well, we know that the two results must add up to white. White is RGB 255/255/255. So, we just subtract our first color from white! Our first color, cyan, was 0/179/179.

RGB 255/255/255 (white) minus RGB 0/179/179 (slightly darkened cyan) = RGB 255/76/76 complementary color (light red).

If these two colors were mixed together, the result would be neutral gray. In this example, we used RGB so the result is white; neutral gray at maximum value. However, if we were mixing paint, the result would be neutral gray, in the subtractive domain, since the mixture would contain 50% of each color. White (full value) times 50% equals neutral gray.

Some Brief Thoughts on Contrast

As I mentioned before, there are many great books written on how to achieve contrasts in your paintings and drawings. I'm not going to spend time covering something that has been covered so thoroughly and so well by others including Itten. However, if you are unfamiliar with the term, contrast and more specifically color contrast is an important element of any design. Think of a symphony; you can't have the loud finale without the quiet parts. Your painting is exactly the same. You need loud parts and quiet parts. You need dynamics. You cannot have light without darkness. You need cool colors in order to bring out the warm ones. You need high value and low value colors, and saturated colors against gray colors. If you want your painting to be alive, you need rhythmic colors and ambient colors...I did say brief, so I'll quit while I'm ahead.

Understanding Color Harmony

As it turns out, understanding color harmony is pretty simple now that we know how the color wheel actually works. You may also want to look in your art box, and if your color wheel shows red and green as complements, this would be a good time to throw it out. That thing will never be of any help. I am shocked at how many supposedly "academic and scholarly" references and websites use an incorrect color wheel. I would go as far as to say most! Back to harmony...

There are several types of color harmonies. The very simplest form is a two-color (dyadic)[2] scheme known as complements. As we have discussed, complementary hues are just two colors opposite each other on the color wheel. We also now know that if one of the colors is a bit on the dark side, the complementary color will be slightly on the light side. We need the colors to combine in the mind (and the palette) to produce a neutral gray, in order to be pleasing to the eye. In addition, we have learned to use a computer to calculate a color's complement.

Analogous Color Harmonies

Another simple binary (dyadic) form of color harmony is a two-color scheme known as analogous colors. This means that the two colors used are immediate neighbors on the color wheel. This scheme can be pleasant but should be used as a last resort. It doesn't have the power to create the same equilibrium in the eye as a complementary or triadic harmony.

Triadic Harmonies – Split Complementaries

---

2. For clarity, many sources incorrectly list a dyadic harmony as one that consists of two colors on a color wheel separated by a space. This is not fully correct! Not to rub it in, but inevitably, they use an incorrect color wheel also. The truth is a dyadic harmony is a two-color scheme (Dyad means pair) which can be analogous, complementary or any other pairing.

Let's move on to a slightly more complex color harmony. This next one is called a triadic harmony. That is to say, we now have three colors in our harmonious scheme. The first triadic harmony we will study is one we call a split complementary. Instead of just using the complementary hue, we will use our first color choice (key color), and the two colors on either side of the complementary color. For example, if we pick red as our key color, the two colors that form a split complementary harmony are cyan/blue and cyan/green. Cyan is the complement, and we leave that one out.

You may have realized by now that all color harmonies are just simple mathematical relationships on the color wheel. Complements are always key color plus 180 degrees (or opposites on the wheel). Split complements are always the key color plus 210 degrees and key color plus 150 degrees. You could even make a triangle where the top points to your key color, and the bottom corners point to the colors on either side of the complement. If you attached it to the color wheel in the center, you could rotate it to show all split complementary harmonies.

There are two general types of triadic harmonies. The first is called an isosceles triadic harmony. This means that two sides of the triangle are of equal length. The split-complementary is a perfect example of this. If your main hue is red (hue 0), your harmony hues would be cyan/blue (hue 210) and cyan/green (hue 150). If you drew a triangle on your color wheel, you would see that two of the sides are of equal length.

The second type of triadic harmony is called an equilateral triadic harmony. This means that all three sides of the triangle are of equal length. If your key hue is red (hue 0), your harmony hues would be blue (hue 240) and green (hue 120). If you drew a triangle on your color wheel, you would see that all three sides are equal length. Of course, these color relationships are maintained as you rotate the harmonic shapes around the color wheel.

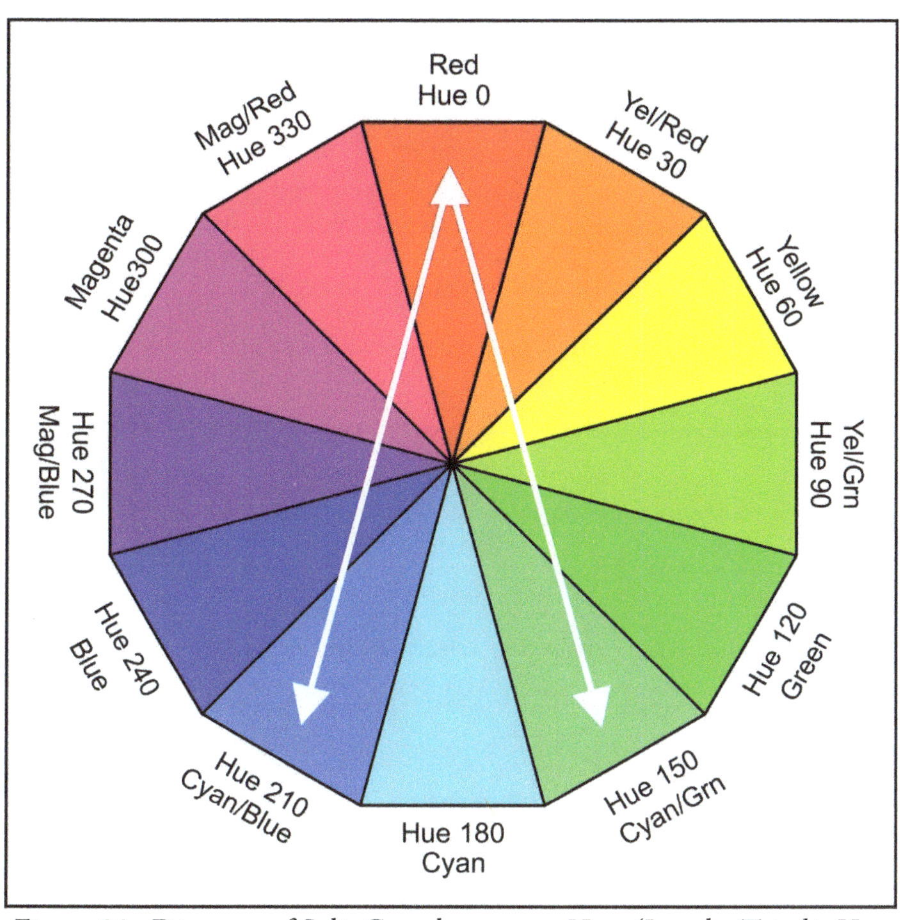

Figure 20 - Diagram of Split Complementary Hues (Isosceles Triadic Harmony)

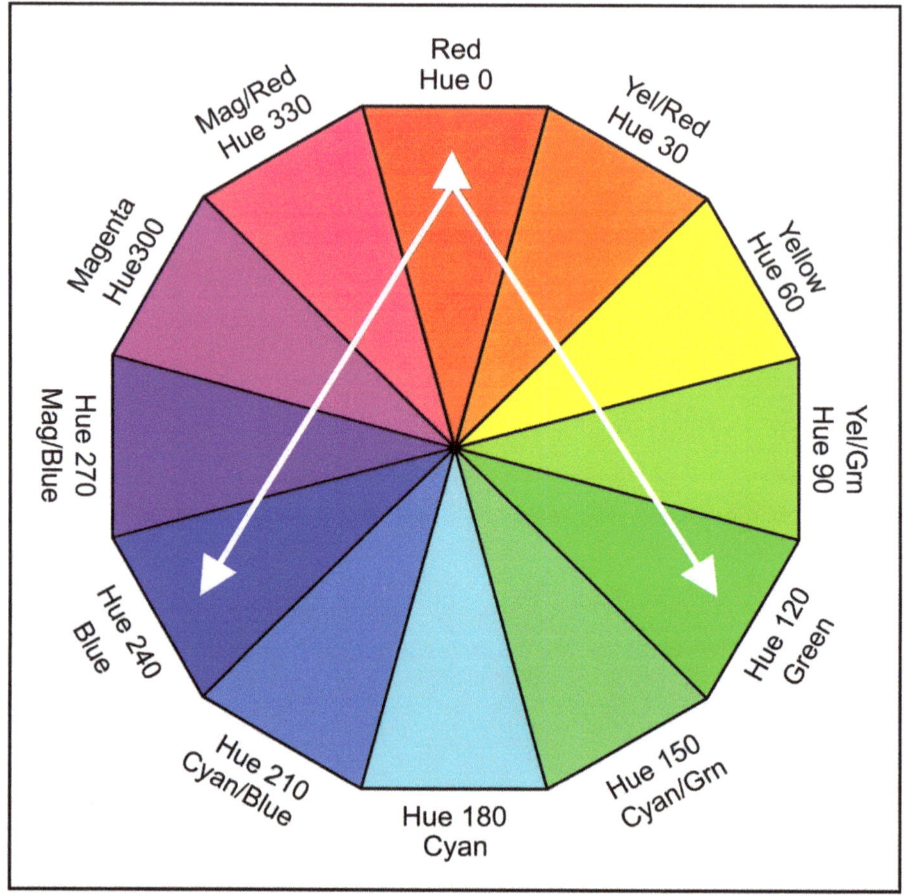

Figure 21 - Diagram of Equilateral Triadic Harmonies

Tetradic Harmonies

Tetradic harmonies are the most complex of all, as they use four colors to create the harmony. There are two general types of tetradic harmonies. The first is called a rectangular tetradic harmony. This means that two sides of the rectangle are of equal length, and the other two sides are of equal length. Here is an example of a rectangular tetradic harmony. If your key hue is magenta/red (hue 330) your harmony hues would be yellow/red (hue 30), and cyan/blue (hue 210) and cyan/green (hue 150). If you drew a rectangle on your color wheel, you would see that two of the sides are of equal length and the other two sides are also equal length, forming a rectangle.

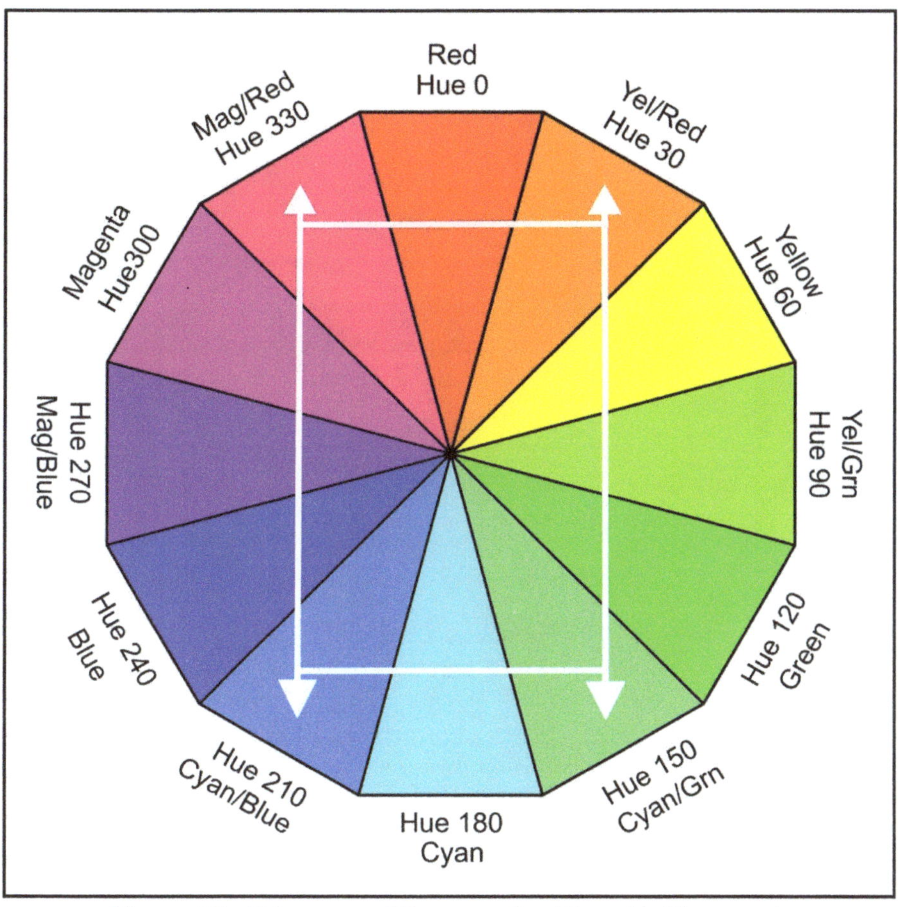

Figure 22– Diagram of Rectangular Tetradic Harmonies

The second type of tetradic harmony is called a square tetradic harmony. Here is an example of a square tetradic harmony. If your key hue is red (hue 0) your harmony hues would be yellow/green (hue 90), cyan (hue 180) and magenta/blue (hue 270). If you drew a square on your color wheel, you would see that all 4 of the sides are of equal length.

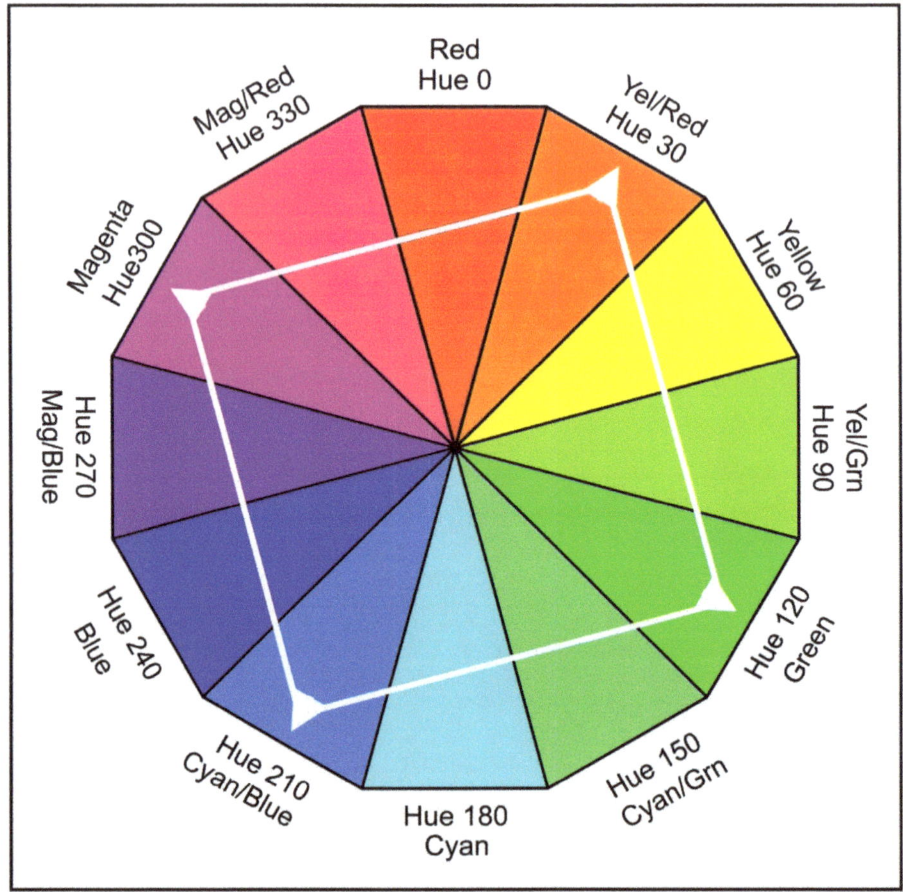

Figure 23 - Diagram of Square Tetradic Harmonies

Some Practical Examples of Theoretical Color Harmonies

In this section, I will show you some examples of sample designs using various theoretical color harmony strategies. Of course, there are hundreds of thousands of possibilities, but this is a good starting point to demonstrate how the mathematical basis for harmony works. You will very quickly become an expert and start experimenting with your own variations and combinations.

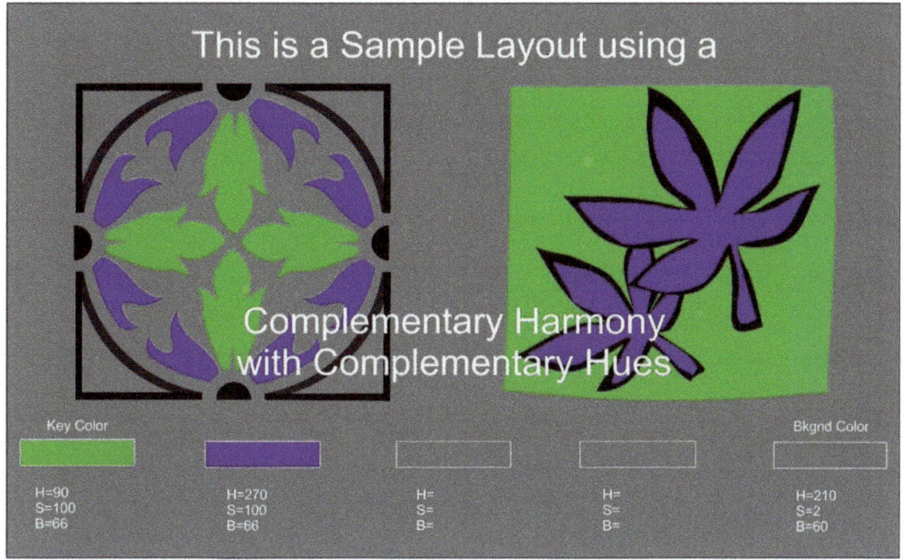

Figure 24 - Complementary Harmony with Complementary Hues

This first example uses the most basic harmony, a dyadic harmony called a complementary pair. For this first example, we are using complementary hues only, not complementary colors. Remember, complementary colors combine to form 50% neutral gray...complementary hues are just opposites on the color wheel and may combine to form any neutral value between black and white. Generally, complementary hues combine to form black when high quality pigments are used. By converting to complementary colors, we guarantee the 50% gray combination, and therefore a balanced eye.

In the sample design, you will see several design elements where I can easily swap the colors to demonstrate the harmony. At the bottom of the sample, I have included color swatches for the harmony colors and listed their HSV numbers. As you recall, the Hue number tells you exactly where the color falls on the circumference of the color wheel. The Saturation tells you the ratio of pure color to gray, and the Value tells you how it compares to a scale of black to white. I have also thrown in some white text, and some other neutral gray elements to simulate an actual design without compromising the color scheme integrity.

The next example uses the same basic dyadic complementary pair. But this time, we are using complementary colors. I lightened the key color a bit and darkened the complementary color in order to achieve the ultimate gray balance. Now when you combine the two colors, either with mixing paint or mixing in your eye, you will achieve 50% neutral gray.

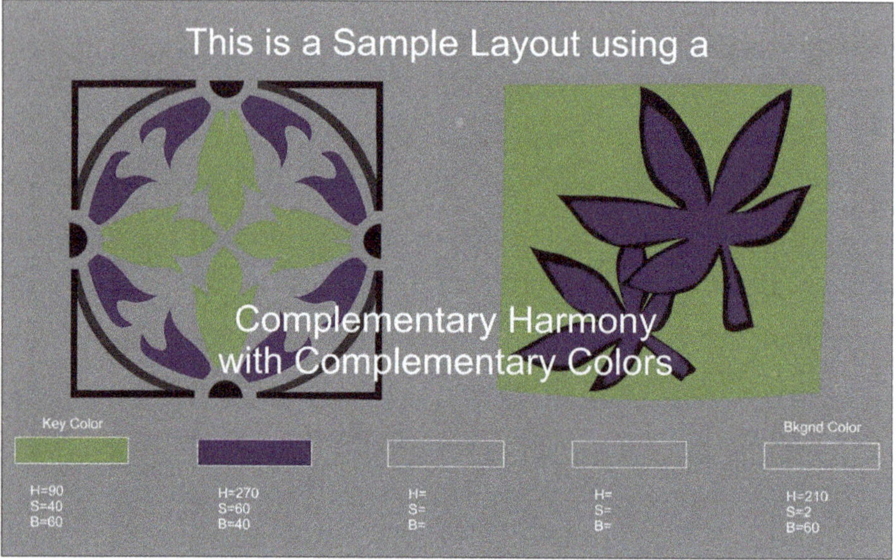

Figure 25 - Complementary Harmony with Complementary Colors

The next example uses a basic triadic scheme called a split complementary. For consistency, I kept the same key color, and instead of the complementary color, I chose the color on either side of the complementary color. This particular scheme relies on the theory that when you use a complementary scheme, your eye receives equal amounts of the three primary colors, through reflected light. By having the colors placed correctly on the color wheel, we also achieve the exact same effect by using a split complement (also called an isosceles triad).

You will notice that in a split complement, instead of having two colors 180 degrees apart, we have a key color, another color 150 degrees from it, and a third color 210 degrees from the key color. You can verify this by looking at the hue numbers for the color swatches.

You may also notice that in the examples, neutral gray shows as hue 210. At close to zero saturation, hue cannot be determined and is completely irrelevant. Therefore, the number for the hue could be anything, and it wouldn't change the color.

For this example I am just using complementary hues to make matters easier to follow. If I were actually designing a painting, I would adjust all of the samples to account for the complementary colors. If my key color is a bit light, I might make my other two a bit darker. I might also adjust the saturation to make the scheme fit the mood of the piece better. You really will master all of these variables fairly quickly and it will become very intuitive. Keep in mind that intuitive knowledge almost always produces better work, but the theory is there as a safe haven when you are feeling a bit lost or directionless.

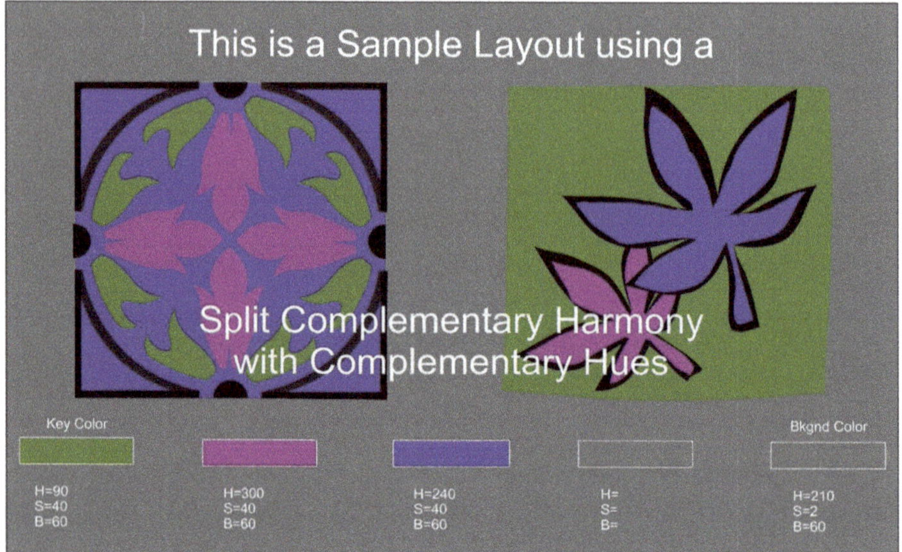

Figure 26 - Split Complementary Harmony with Complementary Hues

In the next example we will use an equilateral triadic harmony, meaning that the two harmony colors are each 120 degrees from the key color, but in opposite directions on the wheel. This also means that all three colors are 120 degrees apart from each other. This particular scheme works on the theory that when you use a triadic complementary scheme, your eye receives equal amounts of the three primary colors, through reflected light.

This is also a great example of the math where I previously mentioned that for some calculations, we need to refer to red as hue 360 instead of 0. If you take hue 90 and add 120 degrees, the result is hue 210. But when you take hue 90 and subtract 120 degrees, you get -30 degrees. Since we don't use negative hue numbers, we just add the result to 360, and we get hue 330 which is the correct answer. You could arrive at the same answer by adding 120 degrees to hue 210 also. Now all three of our hues are 120 degrees apart on the color wheel, which is correct for an equilateral triadic harmony.

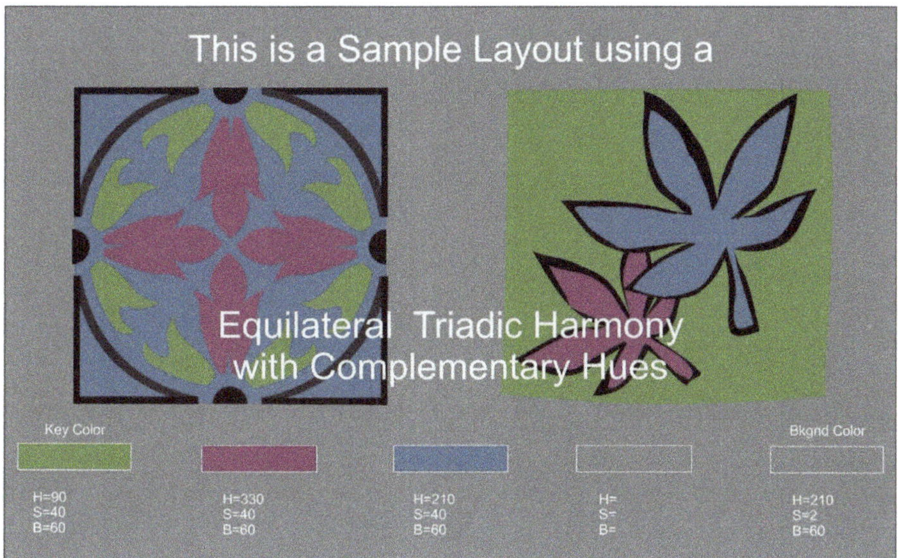

Figure 27 - Equilateral Triadic Harmony with Complementary Hues

Now we will move up in complexity a bit and look at a scheme that uses a rectangular tetradic harmony. In the above example you could imagine a rectangle that starts at hue 90 (yellow green). It then connects to hue 150 (cyan green) and then hue 270 (magenta blue) and finally at hue 330 (magenta red). After that it returns and closes the rectangle at the beginning at hue 90. Of course, once again we are just using the complementary hues to keep the discussion simple. In this particular tetrad, two of the colors are 60 degrees apart at the narrow ends of the rectangle, and the other two are 120 degrees apart on the long sides. This particular scheme can also be thought of as a complementary pair of split complements...in other words, we take a split complement and also split the key color.

By the time we understand these four part color harmonies, you start to get a feel for how powerful even simple harmonies can have dramatic effects on a piece of artwork. I am always shocked and amused by artists that believe they should use every color they own, in every painting. I believe in just using the ones that serve the painting.

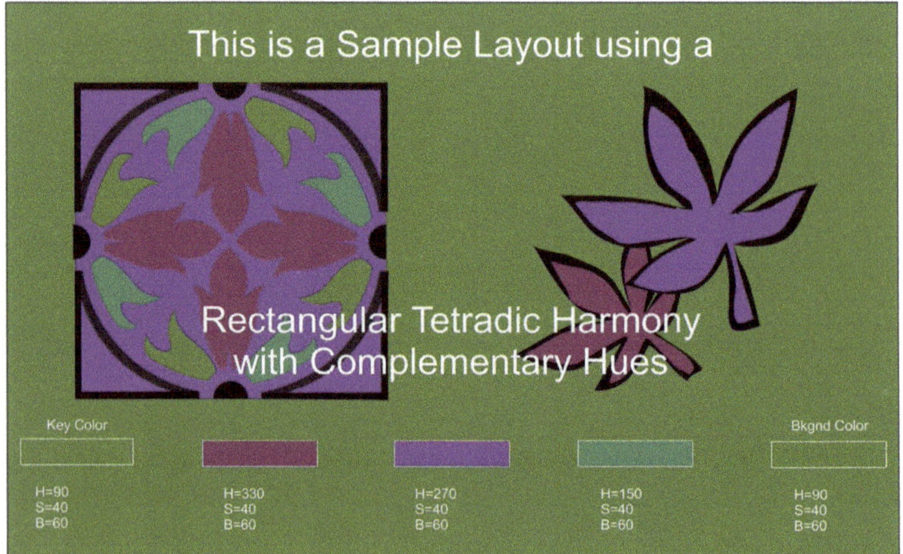

Figure 28 - Rectangular Tetradic Harmony with Complementary Hues

Now we will move up in complexity a bit more and look at a scheme that uses a rectangular tetradic harmony with complementary colors. As we said in the last example this is just a set of split complementary hues...but now we are going to adjust two of the colors to be full complementary colors, to give the eyes that gray balance it desires. This is also the process I would go through when designing the master color scheme for a painting. Of course, this is the process graphic artists, interior designers and in fact, anyone who works with color professionally should be going through.

It may not be completely obvious at this point, so we will recap a bit. The colors at hue 90 and hue 270 are complementary. That is to say that they are 180 degrees apart on the color wheel (90 + 180 = 270). When we are working in the HSB model, the beautifully simple fact is the way to make a complementary color from a complementary hue is to just reverse the Saturation and Brightness numbers on one of them. Our key color is H90 S40 B60 and our complementary hue is H270 S40 B60. So, in order to make this second one into a complementary color we just switch S and B, and it becomes H270 S60 B40!

Exactly the same process applies to our other set of colors located at hue 150 and hue 330. We just swap the S and the B for one half of the pair and they become complementary colors. I could have easily changed the other end of the pair, with the result being that one of the pair becomes a little lighter, and the other is darker, so the total is always 50% gray. It's important to think of this process as a scale, if you get a bit heavy on the darks, add some lights to keep it balanced. These are the decisions you make as an artist.

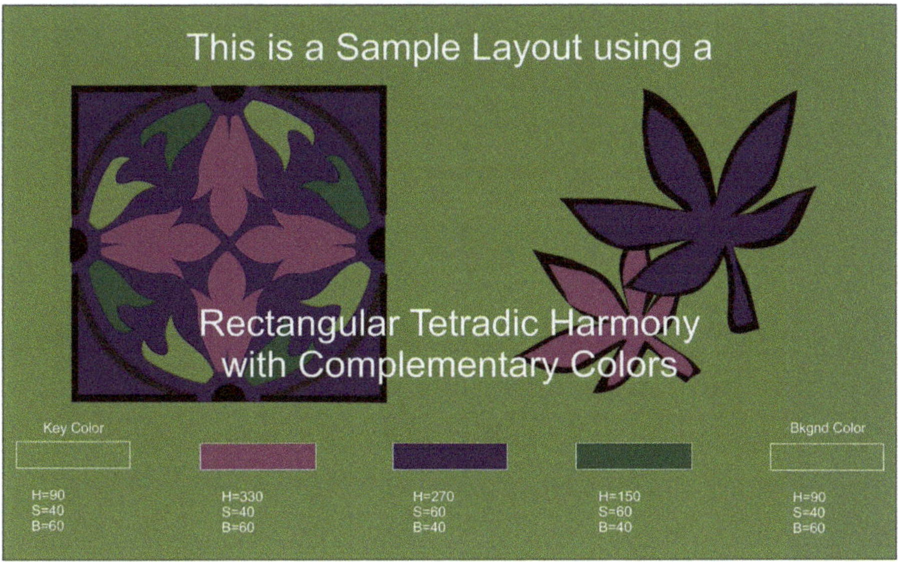

Figure 29 - Rectangular Tetradic Harmony with Complementary Colors

Now we will look at a scheme that uses a square tetradic harmony. In the example you could imagine a square that starts at hue 90 (yellow green). It then connects to hue 180 (cyan) and then hue 270 (magenta blue) and finally at hue 0 (red). After that it returns and closes the rectangle at the beginning at hue 90. Of course, we are just using the complementary hues to keep the discussion simple. In this particular tetrad, all of the colors are 90 degrees apart from each other. This is a fairly common theoretical color scheme, and we will see it used it in the next several examples.

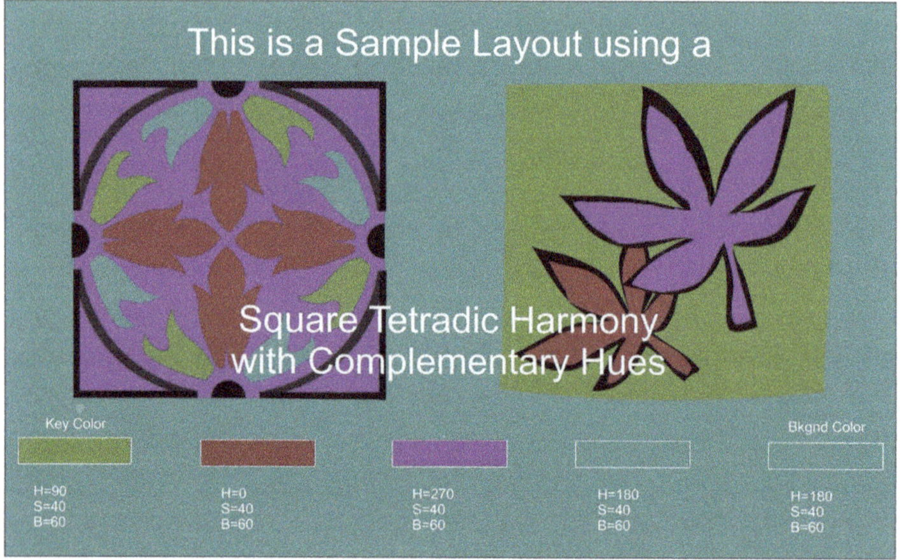

Figure 30 - Square Tetradic Harmony with Complementary Hues

In the examples below, I will take the exact same square tetradic harmony used in the example above and modify it slightly to show some the possibilities. In the first example I have maintained the same tetradic relationships but just shifted them around the color wheel. To do this I simply added 75 degrees to all of the hue numbers. In the next example I did exactly the same thing, but I added 125 degrees to all of the hue numbers. After that, the exact same color formula with 215 degrees added to the hue numbers. In essence, all four examples are the same color formula, but just rotated around the color wheel.

For the fifth example, I got a little fancy. I changed the hue by adding 75 degrees, but I also subtracted 50% from the saturation numbers. This grayed the design down a bit and gave it more of an uptown feel. It's interesting how just decreasing the saturation a bit makes the scheme look much more expensive and higher end when it's the same design. Now that I've given you a lot to digest, it's time to get out your paints and experiment. At least get out your laptop and play with a color program.

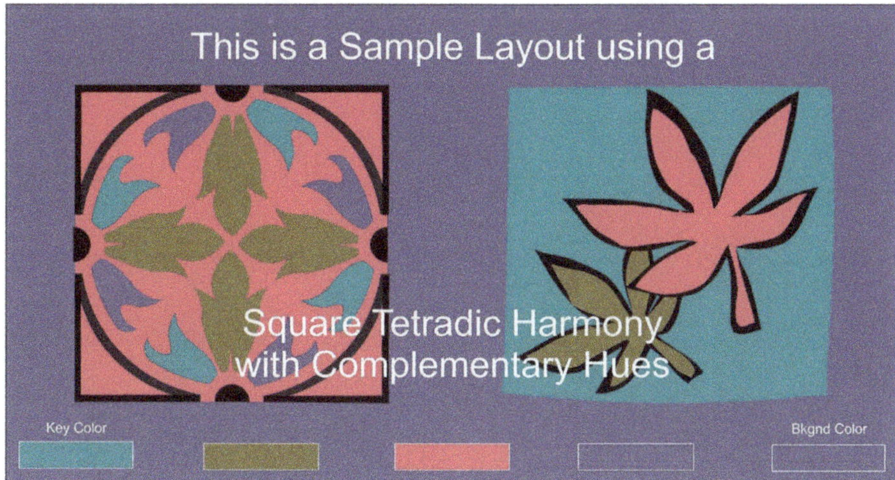

Figure 31 - Square Tetradic Harmony with Complementary Hues Hue +75 Degrees

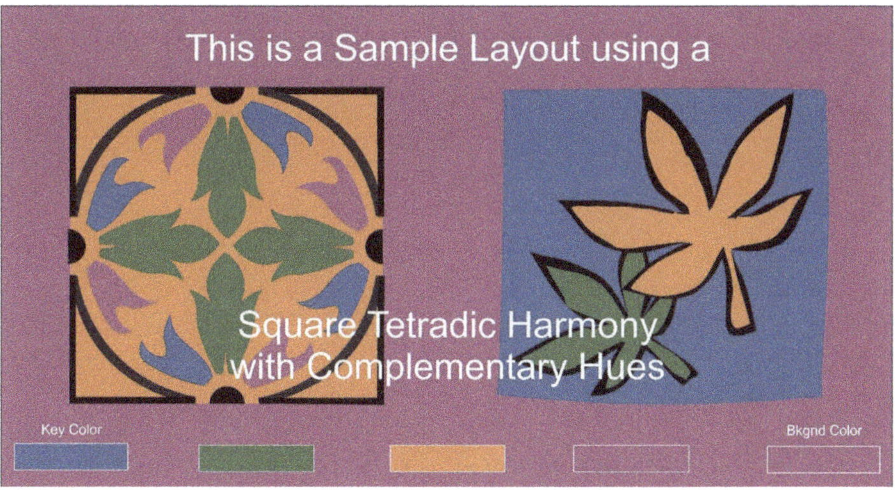

Figure 32 - Square Tetradic Harmony with Complementary Hues Hue +125 Degrees

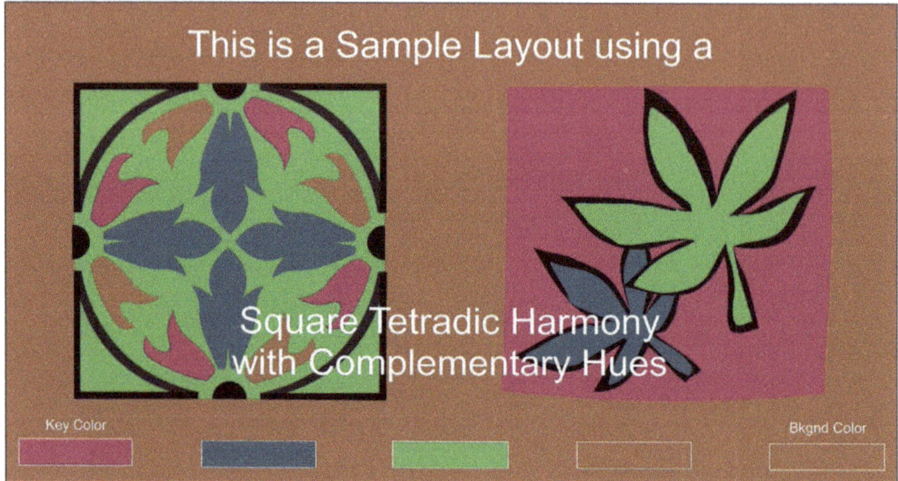

Figure 33 - Square Tetradic Harmony with Complementary Hues Hue +215 Degrees

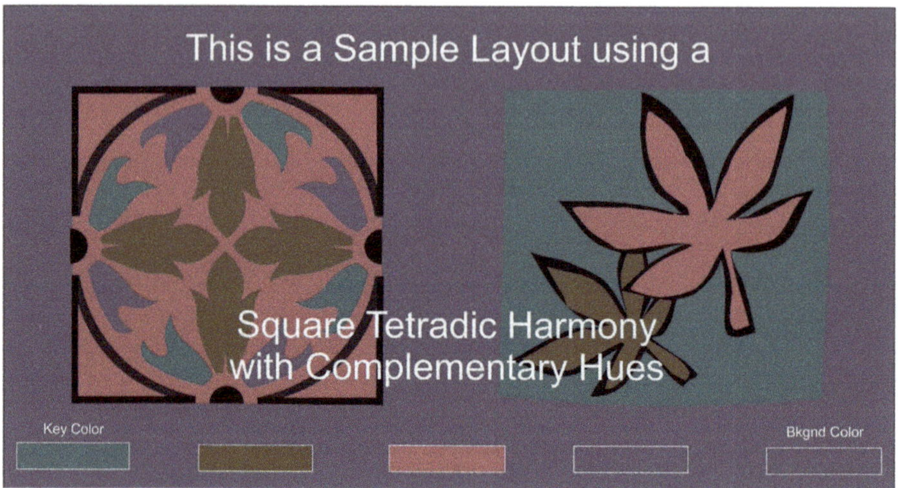

Figure 34 - Square Tetradic Harmony with Complementary Hues and Hue +75 Degrees and Saturation - 50%

That completes our discussion of color harmonies. It's all about simple mathematical relationships. After a while you will be able to visualize the relationships, but in the meanwhile, don't be afraid to cut out the geometric shapes, and pin them to your color wheel. Also think about balancing the eye. If one of your colors is a bit dark, make the other one or two a bit light. If one is grayed down, make the other one similarly grayed down. Play around with these ideas and it won't be long before you are a master of color harmony. If you would like to follow along with these examples, please see the notes in the chapter on "Using a Computer to Study Color" for some helpful suggestions.

CHROMA SUTRA

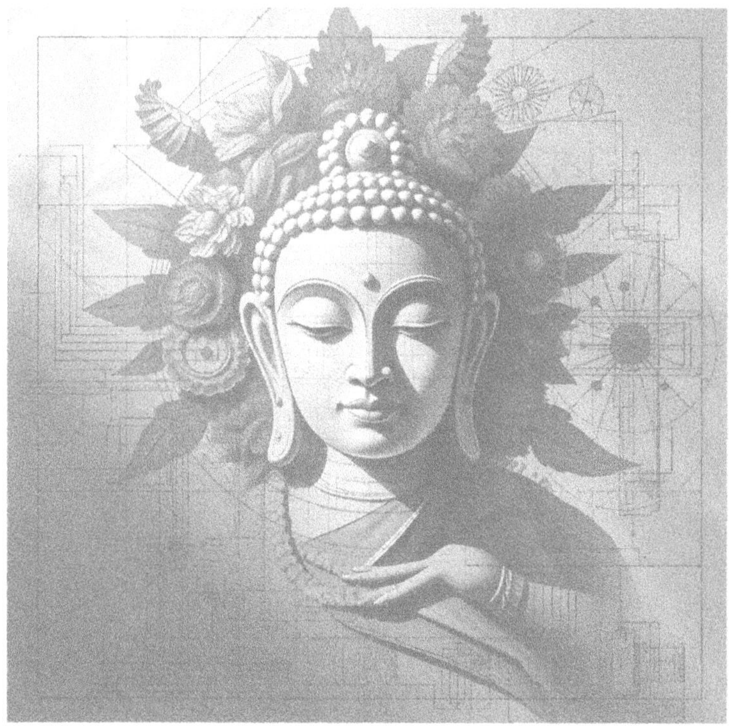

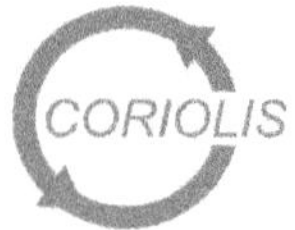

Chapter 8
A Practical Painting Palette

We have now learned that a painting palette can be set up using just three colors, and white. Magenta, primary yellow, cyan and white. Virtually any color can easily be mixed from this set of four pigments. In fact, if you see a color you really like in a book or magazine, it was made by mixing these three colors. If I were a plein air (outdoor) painter, traveling light, I would be able to use this setup without any reservations. Is this the palette I use every day in my studio? The answer is yes and no. So, I would like to go into the details of why I use the colors I use. But first, a plug for Maimeri...

As I have mentioned previously, the quality of the paint makes a dramatic difference in the results you will obtain. I only use paint made by Maimeri. Maimeri is not my sponsor, I have no affiliation with them. I recommend it because they make the highest quality paint. They are the only brand I have used where the pigments behave according to the laws of color theory, consistently and reliably. When you mix yellow and blue you get black. Mix cyan and red you get black. Mix green and magenta, you get black. Also, they are not the most expensive. They make two grades of paint: One is called "Classico," which they consider a student grade paint (however, that is the one I use most). The second is called "Puro" which is more expensive but is nothing short of incredible. To be honest, the only time I use Puro is when I am trying to match a color exactly, and I have spent more than a few minutes without the success I'm looking for using the Classico. I should add, this is quite rare. I would say in the last two years of painting daily, there were only three times I had to reach for the Puro, out of tens of thousands of color mixes. I'm sure there must be other brands with great paint, and most artists have brands they swear by. I only mention this because if you want to guarantee success in learning correct color theory, you can't go wrong with Maimeri. If you want to experiment with other brands, I encourage it! If you are just starting out though, take the easy way out!

The Holland Ten Color Palette, and How I Got There

Now, back to my practical palette. When I paint daily, in my studio, I lay out 10 colors, in this order: Magenta, cadmium red medium, yellow ochre, cadmium yellow deep, thalo blue-green, Prussian blue, burnt umber, titanium white, mars black and sludge bistre. (I actually formulate my own white and bistre, but more on that later). From these 10, I have only rarely found a color I couldn't match very quickly, and even then it was so close one needs to question one's criticality.

Let's now examine how we went from three colors plus white, to nine colors plus white. If I were in the field doing plein air, I would start with a tube of primary yellow, cyan and magenta, along with the titanium white. I would be able to make any color I needed, and with a little bit of alkyd resin medium, I could even do glazing. So, what is the drawback, and why not always use this palette? There are two reasons to increase to a six color palette. The three primaries, cyan, magenta and primary yellow, tend to be very transparent. This has multiple benefits, but also some drawbacks; sometimes you don't want the colors to be so transparent. Now, if you create a tint by adding white (which is very common) the color will of course be opaque, so that solves a lot of the problem. The second problem is that many color mixes require you to add all three primaries together in various combinations. If you start with one primary, it is faster to add a color that already contains the other two primaries. As an example, if you start with yellow and you want the mix to be more blue, you could add cyan and magenta, or you could add blue. The result is the same, but the second method is faster.

I'll explain a bit more: Let's look at our three color palette and the evolution to six colors. I started with magenta, primary yellow and cyan. I ended up with magenta, cadmium yellow deep and thalo blue green. What was my thinking? The magenta is perfect (slightly transparent) but I can work with that. The yellow is very transparent, so I swap that for cadmium yellow deep. The cadmium yellow follows the theory well and is less transparent. If I ever need the transparency, I have the primary yellow in the paint box. So, why the thalo blue green? The cyan is fine and will work in most situations; however, according to the color theory, cyan should be exactly halfway between blue and green. I find that in practice, the thalo blue green is closer to theoretically perfect than the cyan, but they are really close, and it may just be a personal preference. To get to the six color palette, I add yellow ochre, cadmium red medium and Prussian blue.

We know that yellow ochre is just a mix of yellow and magenta. Cadmium red is just magenta and yellow. Prussian blue is just a mix of magenta and cyan. So why add these? Well, all of these colors are more opaque, so when you mix with these, the transparency problems are reduced. In addition, these are all combinations of two primaries, which save time in three color mixes. If I start with yellow and I need to add blue, I reach for the Prussian blue. I get exactly the same result by adding magenta and cyan but I save time. Now on to the next four colors.

I also include mars black and burnt umber. These are two colors I could easily mix from our primaries but why bother when I use them a lot. It is much faster to squirt them out of a tube, and it leaves me more time to paint. The last two colors are more complicated and not entirely necessary, but they save me time and eliminate waste. The first is what I call alkyd titanium white. It is not an alkyd based paint, but regular titanium white oil paint. I grind it to a much finer consistency than normal and add alkyd resin and put it in tubes. This produces a really fine white that also has the benefit of making everything dry much more quickly. Mostly personal preference, but I don't have to add the resin to every color I mix. The last color I use is sludge bistre. Normally, this is the sludge at the bottom of your can of brush cleaner. Instead, when I'm finished painting I collect all the unused paint and put it in a jar. I save it, stir it up, process it and put it in tubes for later use. This bistre is neutral gray and the perfect color to use for graying down colors and making tones. As a bonus, I end up with nearly a zero paint waste studio. I hope this explains the practical decisions I made to come up with this ideal palette. I would encourage you to give it a try. In the beginning just use titanium white and a good neutral gray, you don't have to start by mixing your own.

In the next section, I will show the Holland Ten Color palette with the Maimeri Classico tube colors and my own sludge bistre. That will be followed by some color charts I made.

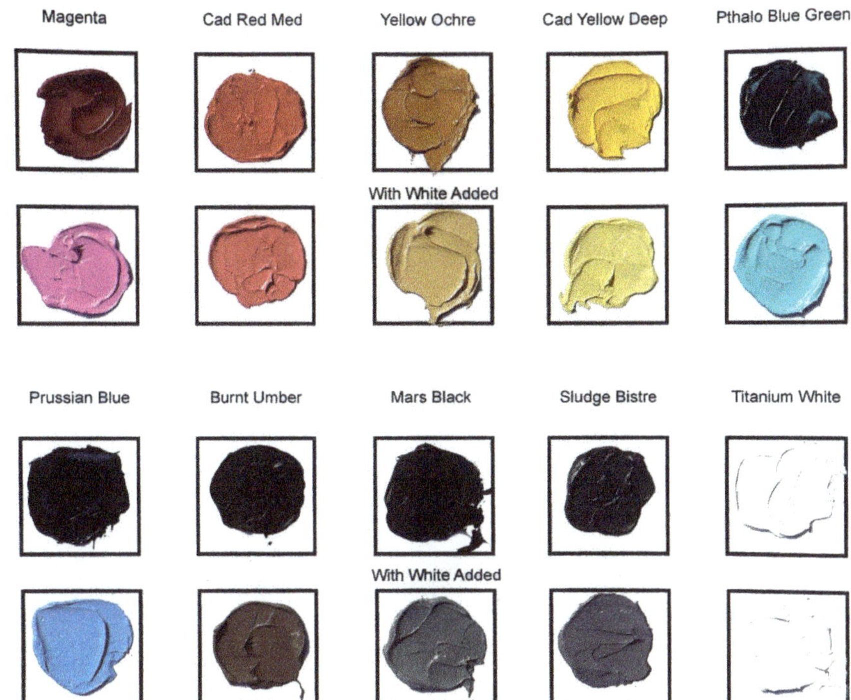

The Holland Ten Color Painting Palette (using Maimeri Classico)

CHROMA SUTRA

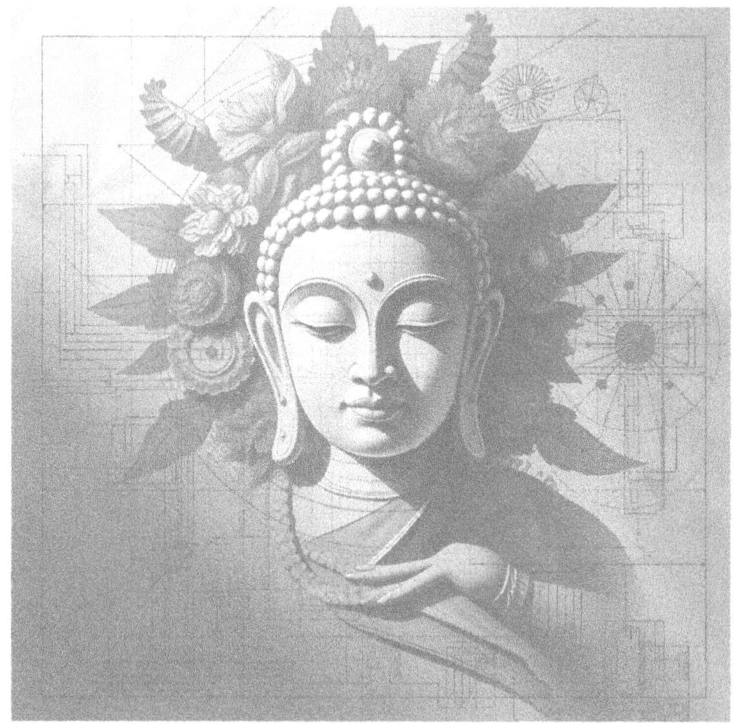

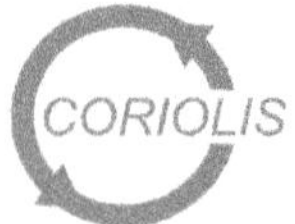

Chapter 9
Some General Reference Materials

The following section includes a set of eight test panels I made for the Holland Ten Color Palette. These were made using Maimeri Classico oils, the ones I paint with daily. Each panel has the name of one of the eight tube colors. Across the top of the panel is the name of the other colors in the palette. That is followed by several tints of the main hue to demonstrate the potential range of the mixtures.

Each chart is labeled with the main color it represents, mixed with the other tube colors. As an example, on the magenta panel, we start in the upper left hand corner with each of the eight colors being mixed with magenta. Can you predict where this is going? Correct...the first square is magenta mixed with magenta, yielding, you guessed it, magenta. Then the next is cadmium red mixed with magenta, yellow ochre mixed with magenta and so on. As we work down the panel, we see each of those mixtures with progressively more white added, with the bottom row containing the most white in the mixture. All of the mixtures except the top row are tints of the main mixtures.

Adding white to a color does several things. First, it obviously creates a lighter tint, but it also reduces the transparency dramatically. In addition, it acts as a "truth detector." Let me explain. Many of the tube colors are quite dark, which makes it difficult to judge the accuracy of your mixes.

You can see this to some degree in the color wheel I mixed up. By adding just a bit of white to a small amount off to the side, it makes it easier to see how close your mix really is. Is it too magenta? Too cyan? Too yellow? Keep asking yourself those three questions! You can also ask yourself the nine questions in Bob Dylan's "Blowin' in the Wind", but I digress.

At the time I made those color panels, I was using cadmium lemon as my main yellow. It's a great choice, but my new preference is cadmium yellow deep. It just works better for the style of painting I'm doing at the moment. I may revert at some time; I keep several yellows in my paintbox. You will likely experiment and develop your own preferences.

To summarize, I want to restate a few of my personal preferences to avoid confusion. I still do all of my mixing using the three-color (cyan, magenta and yellow) principles. I use the magenta out of the tube, it works perfectly! However, I prefer thalo blue green to the standard cyan and use them interchangeably. They are so close very few people would even see a difference, but I find it nearer to theoretically perfect since it is exactly halfway between blue and green. Lastly, instead of primary yellow, which works great for theoretical mixes and glazing, I had found at that time, I preferred cadmium lemon for my actual painting. It's very close, but less transparent. After many years of use, I have now switched to cadmium yellow deep. Once again, extremely close, and still performs according to theory, but more suited to my current style. Just personal preferences, and you likely will develop your own. If you are heavily involved in glazing (that is building up layers of transparent colors) you likely will prefer the original cyan (or thalo blue green), magenta and primary yellow. I would also encourage you to make your own set of test panels like these. They can be thought of as a color recipe book. They are a handy resource, and great mixing practice. The more time and accuracy you put into them, the more valuable a resource they will become.

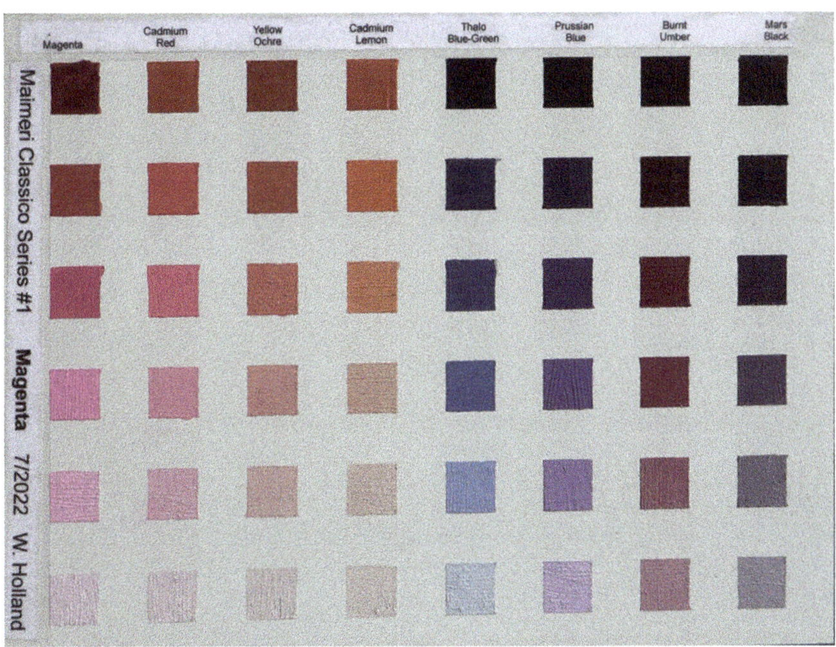

Figure 36 - Maimeri Classico Magenta Test Panel

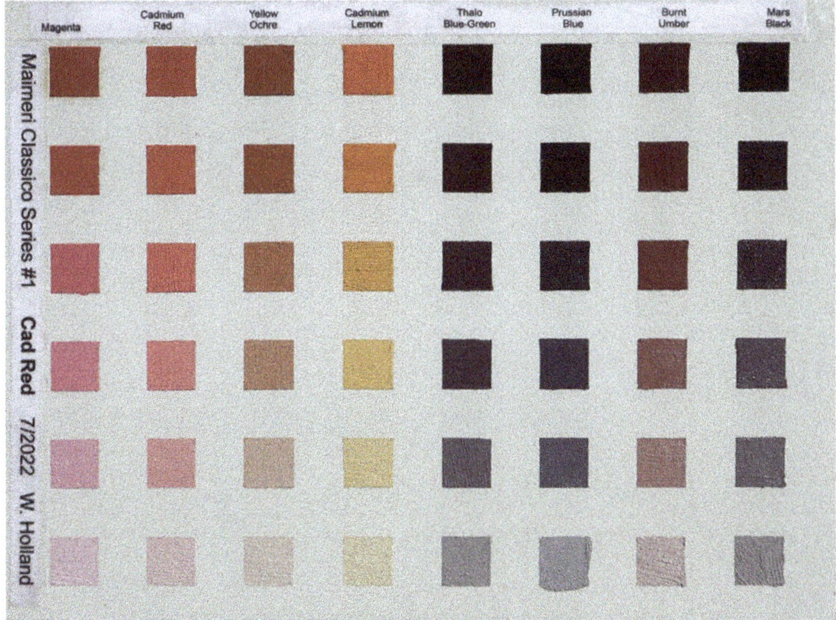

Figure 37 - Maimeri Classico Cad Red Test Panel

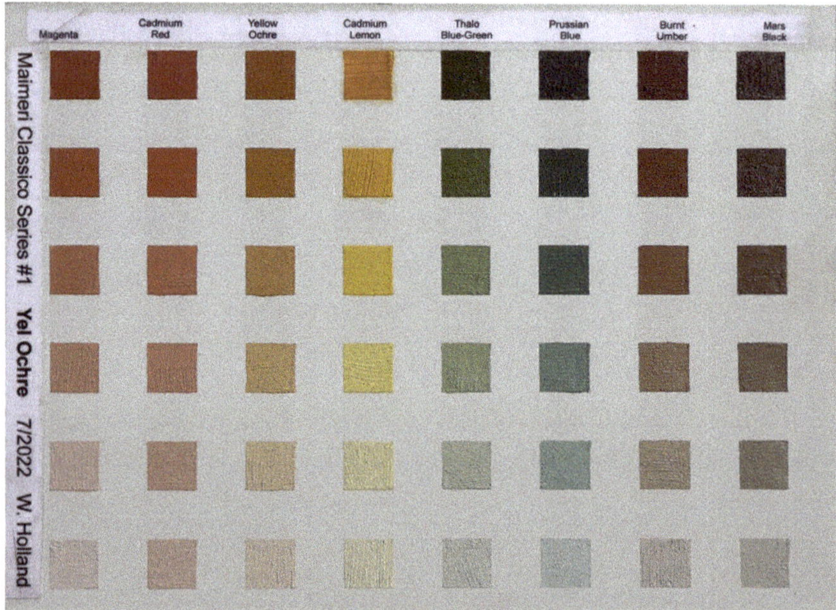

Figure 38 - Maimeri Classico Yellow Ochre Test Panel

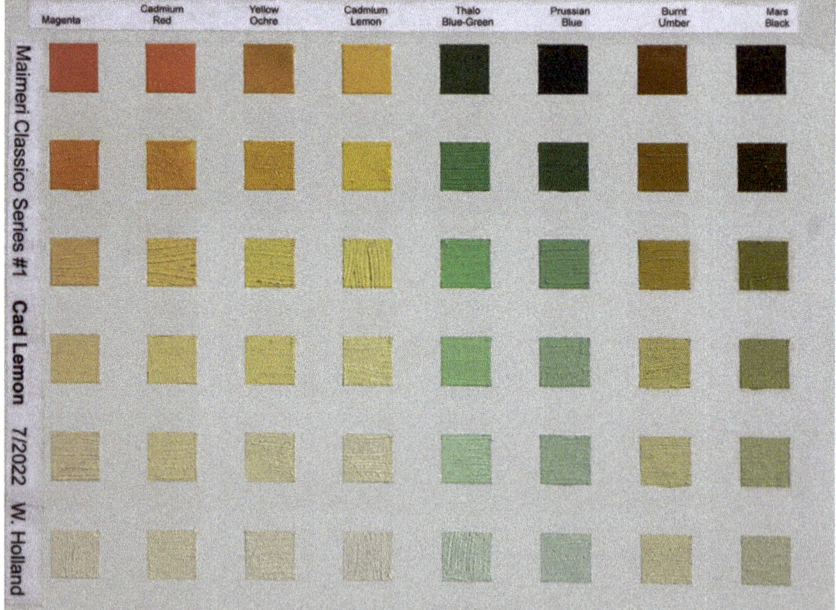

Figure 39 - Maimeri Classico Cadmium Lemon Test Panel

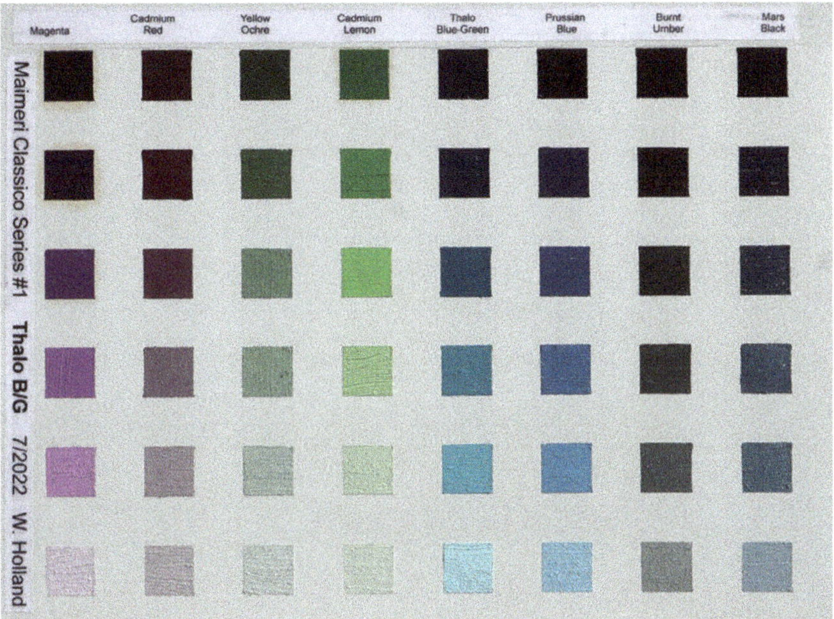

Figure 40 - Maimeri Classico Thalo Blue/ Green Test Panel

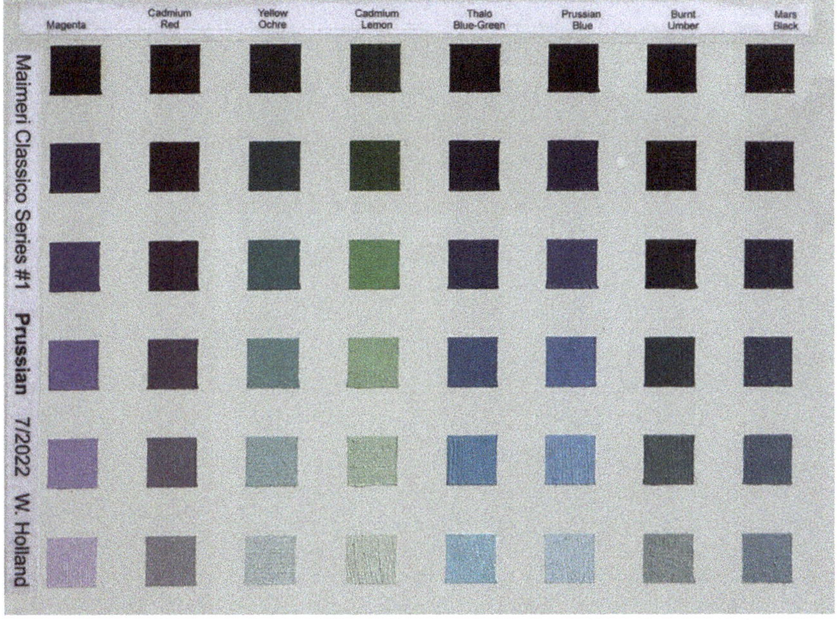

Figure 41 - Maimeri Classico Prussian Blue Test Panel

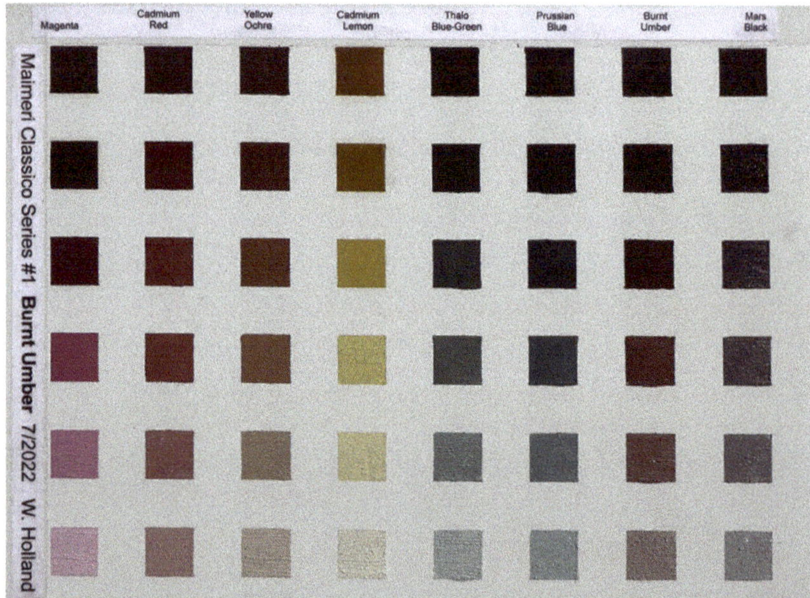

Figure 42 - Maimeri Classico Burnt Umber Test Panel

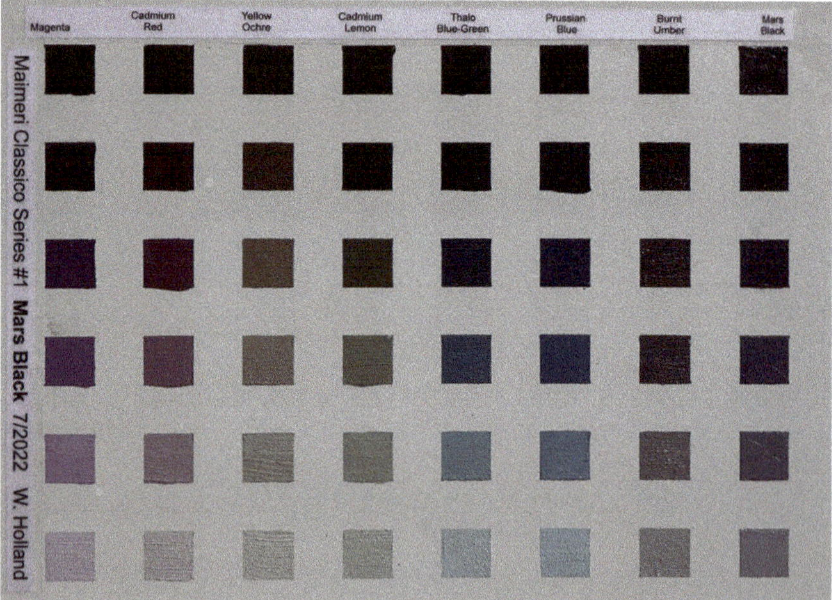

Figure 43 - Maimeri Classico Mars Black Test Panel

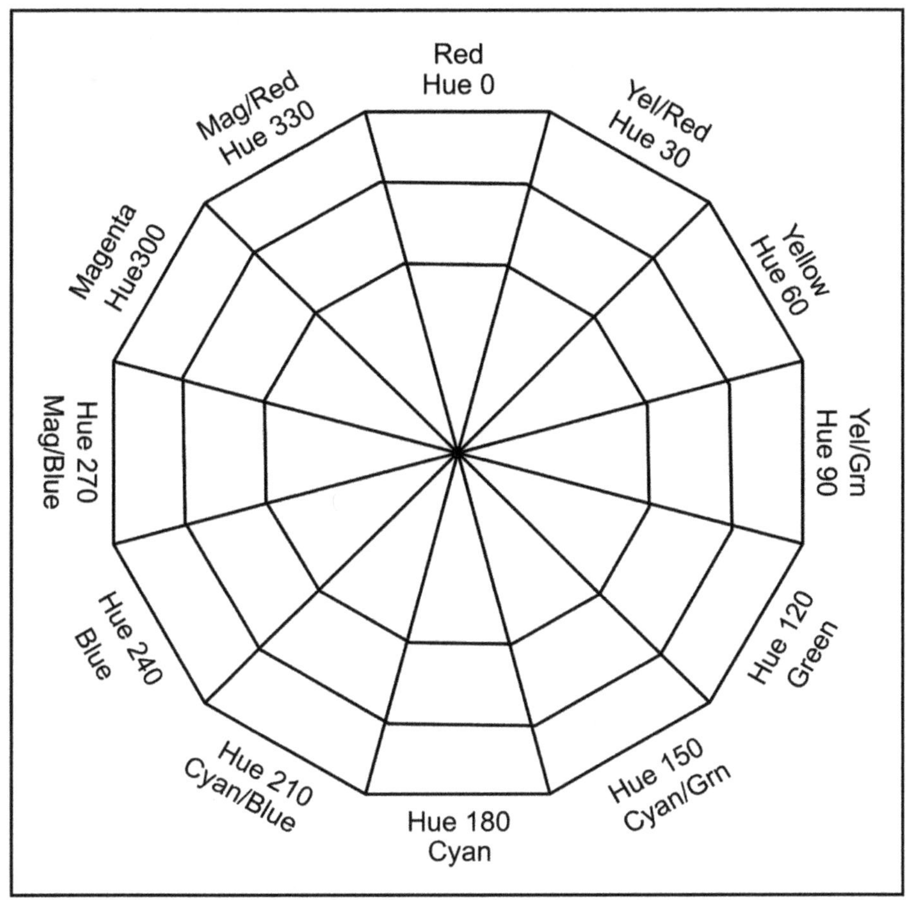

Figure 44 - Blank Color Wheel for Student Use

CHROMA SUTRA

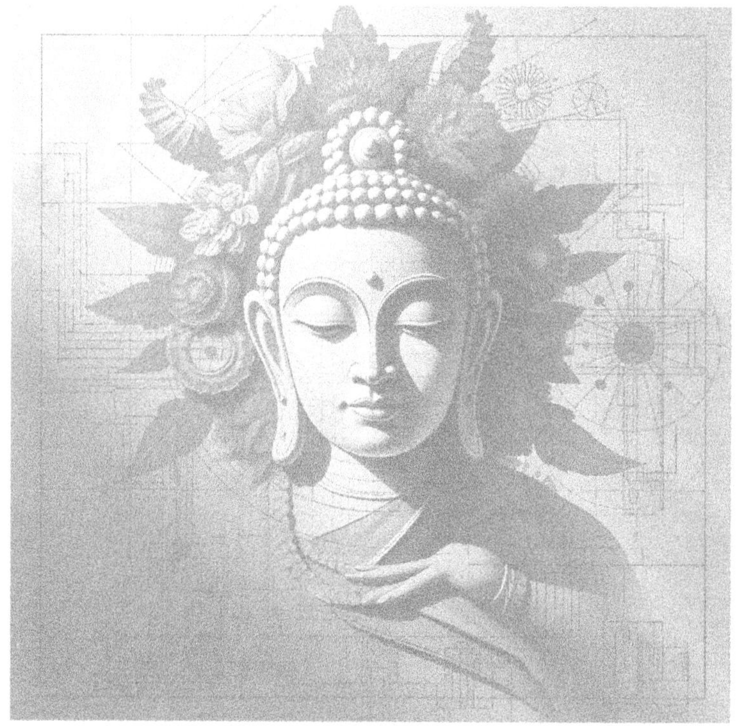

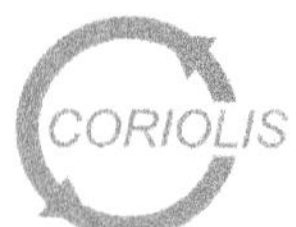

Chapter 10
Using a Computer to Study Color

Why Should I Use a Computer if I am a Traditional Artist?

A computer can be a marvelous tool for any artist studying color. You can use it to analyze and measure the properties of a particular color, mix a color until it is to your liking, or even calculate the entire color palette for a design. You can sample and analyze the colors in a photo or existing design and use the data to establish a new color palette. This doesn't even begin to cover all the timesaving uses for artists that create digital art or do design work, packaging, CAD/CAM (computer aided design and manufacturing) and even use AI (Artificial Intelligence) to spark ideas. The computer has become an absolutely indispensable tool for the modern artist. Even if you are a purist and don't want the computer directly involved in your work, you may have a website or use it to file and archive photos of your work. You may manage your art business and finances or simply document your growth and progress.

Some Notes About Color Specification Systems

I have mentioned the different systems used for specifying colors in art and industry. Some of them are extremely complex. I would say that the complexity of the system and the usefulness for artists is probably inversely proportional. However, the systems that you are likely to see on the computer are very straightforward, namely RGB (red, green, blue), CMYK (cyan, magenta, yellow and black) and HSV or HSL (hue, saturation and value or hue, saturation and lightness). I would like to spend a moment talking about the differences.

We have spent considerable time discussing HSV. I don't want to dwell on this since as artists, you are familiar with this method by now. However, a quick recap: Hue is just the location around the circumference of the color wheel, stated in degrees from 0 to 360. Saturation represents the ratio of pure color to neutral gray. Value is where the lightness or darkness of the color falls on a scale of black to white.

RGB is a distinctive way of specifying colors since it is generally used for additive color mixing; that is when mixing light. It is quite simple and elegant though. Each of the additive primaries are represented by a number between 0 and 255. (This is a holdover from computer programming, since colors are typically represented by a 24-bit number, with each primary color being 8 bits). With 8 bits, you get 256 values or 0-255. An RGB color looks like this: R0, G0, B255. This would be the brightest full blue, or blue at maximum intensity. If we want full max yellow, the number would be R255, G255, B0. As the numbers get smaller, the color gets darker, since there is less light. The bigger the numbers, the closer to white. When all three numbers are equal a neutral gray is produced (for example, 0, 0, 0 is black, and 255, 255, 255 is white, 127, 127, 127 is 50% neutral gray).

Sometimes you will see colors represented by a system called CMYK. This stands for Cyan, Magenta, Yellow and Black. This system is designed to be used for artwork that will ultimately be printed on a printing press or some type of inkjet or other technology. In this system, which is exclusively used for specifying subtractive primaries, the colors are listed in percentages. C100, M0, Y100, K0 would be fire engine red. If printers all used really good ink, we would only need the first three colors. However, most printing processes benefit from the addition of black ink to beef up the dark colors a bit. Also, for things like black text, it's easier to skip the first three colors altogether. It's pretty easy to convert between these three systems at the time of creation, so when you get ready to deliver your final work, be sure to ask what format the printer or manufacturer needs.

A Useful Tool for Studying Color Harmony

Many years ago, I designed a simple tool for studying color harmony (See figure 45). I call it "Computer Color Assistant." I shared it with my students, and frankly I'm a little surprised at how useful it has been over the years, and how I still use it regularly some 40 years later. I will give you a simple description and tell you how to make your own so you can have one to use on your computer.

I start with a background of 50% neutral gray, since this is an ideal backdrop for color mixing. You can easily compare colors in terms of hue, saturation and value against a neutral background. This is also why many painters use a mixing palette that consists of a sheet of glass that has been painted neutral gray on the back (Free advice: don't buy a ready-made. Go to your local glass shop, ask for a piece of quarter-inch thick tempered glass the size you want, and spray paint the back neutral gray). Now back to the "Computer Color Assistant."

Next, I have two large rectangles at the top. The first is called the "key" color. That is the color you have chosen as the first part of your harmonious palette. Directly beneath that I have placed the complementary color, that is the color directly across from the key color on the color wheel. Right below that I have two more rectangles that represent the split complements. They are the colors directly across the color wheel on either side of the formal complement. This is also called an isosceles triadic harmony. Below that, I have two more rectangles representing the equilateral triadic harmony. Finally, below that we have two more sets of four rectangles representing the rectangular and square tetradic harmonies.

So here are some interesting observations about the various colored rectangles: In the first two (the complements) we have the key color (the red one at the top) set to hue = 0. Keep in mind that the hue number is just the number of degrees around the color wheel with red at the top being "0". The complement of course is (key color + 180 hue). Hue 0 + 180 = hue 180 or cyan. For the split complementary pair instead of hue = 180, we take that number and add 30 to one and subtract 30 from the other. That leaves us with hue = 210 for the first one and hue = 150 for the second one. The reason for this is that our colors on the wheel are 30 degrees of hue apart, and a split complementary doesn't use the complement, but uses the color on either side of the complement. In this case, cyan/blue and cyan/green.

For our other triadic harmony, the equilateral triadic, all of the colors are equally spaced around the wheel, so at 120 degrees apart we get red, green and blue, which happen to be the subtractive secondaries and the additive primaries.

And for our last two sets of tetradic harmonies, we have the square and rectangular tetradics. You may notice that the rectangular tetradic is just two sets of split complements, and the square is two separate pairs of complements. I should mention that with the complement and the triadic harmonies, don't forget to include the key color! For the tetradic harmonies, you will see that the key color is built in. I would like to reiterate that the purpose of every one of these harmonies is to stimulate the eye with equal amounts of the primary colors to form a neutral gray (somewhere between black and white). Something like what Itten[1] was trying to do...

Now here are the details of how to construct your own version. Use any drawing, layout, publishing, CAD or painting program that lets you output your file as a JPG. I used Photoshop, but many other programs are equally adequate. Start with a neutral gray background by filling your document with RGB 127/127/127. This tells you the amount of Red, Green and Blue respectively. Anytime the three numbers are equal, you have neutral gray. The smaller numbers are darker, and the larger numbers are lighter. The numbers range from 0-255, which is derived from a binary number in the software. The halfway point is actually 127.5, so sometimes you will see 127 or 128 because of rounding errors.

Now draw your 14 rectangular boxes in roughly the same places I have done in the first chart below. You can also use the text command to label all the boxes with their correct harmonic function. The last step is to fill each box with the correct color. Use the color picking tool in the RGB mode to assign the colors. Set the color picker to the value RGB 255/0/0. This should give you pure red; use it to fill the key color rectangle. Next set the color picker to RGB 0/255/255 which is cyan. Fill the box labeled "complement." For the split complementaries, fill the first box with RGB

---

1. Itten got a lot of things right, but the issue is that if your colors are in the wrong positions on the color wheel, the geometry no longer matters. You still end up with the wrong answer.

0/127/255, and the second one with RGB 0/255/128. For the triadic harmonies, fill the first box with RGB 0/0/255, and the second one with RGB 0/255/0. For the square tetradic harmonies, fill the first box with RGB 255/0/0, and the second one with RGB 128/255/0. Fill the third box with RGB 0/255/255, and the fourth one with RGB 128/0/255. For the rectangular tetradic harmonies, fill the first box with RGB 255/0/0, and the second one with RGB 0/255/0. Fill the third box with RGB 0/255/255, and the fourth one with RGB 255/0/255. Now that your diagram looks just like mine, save the file as a JPG. Give it a name you will remember like "Computer Color Assistant."

One of the ways to use this chart is to open the file in a program like Photoshop that allows you to adjust colors. This time you are going to select "adjust hue." I'm going to add 60 to the hue, and therefore rotate my entire diagram 60 degrees around the color wheel. If you look at the second diagram, my key color is yellow, which is red + 60 degrees. You will notice that the complement, blue, is also shifted by 60 degrees. In fact, every color on my chart is now shifted by 60 degrees, but the harmonic relationships all remain the same. You can change the hue, saturation and value of the document, and all of the harmonic relationships stay the same. This is a very easy and powerful tool for developing color harmonies. Just a note: when you are changing the color relationships but you want the background to stay neutral gray, just use the select tool (magic wand icon) to select only the colored boxes. Then only the colors will change. When you have created your new altered color palette, don't forget to rename the file when you save it, to preserve your original "Computer Color Assistant."

In the third chart, I have rotated the hue 120 degrees making my key color green and the complement magenta. For the fourth chart, I have lightened the entire color scheme by adding 50% to the Value number. And finally, for the fifth chart, I have darkened the entire color scheme by subtracting 75% from the Value number. I think with a bit of experimentation you will find this a very useful way to try color combinations quickly and efficiently.

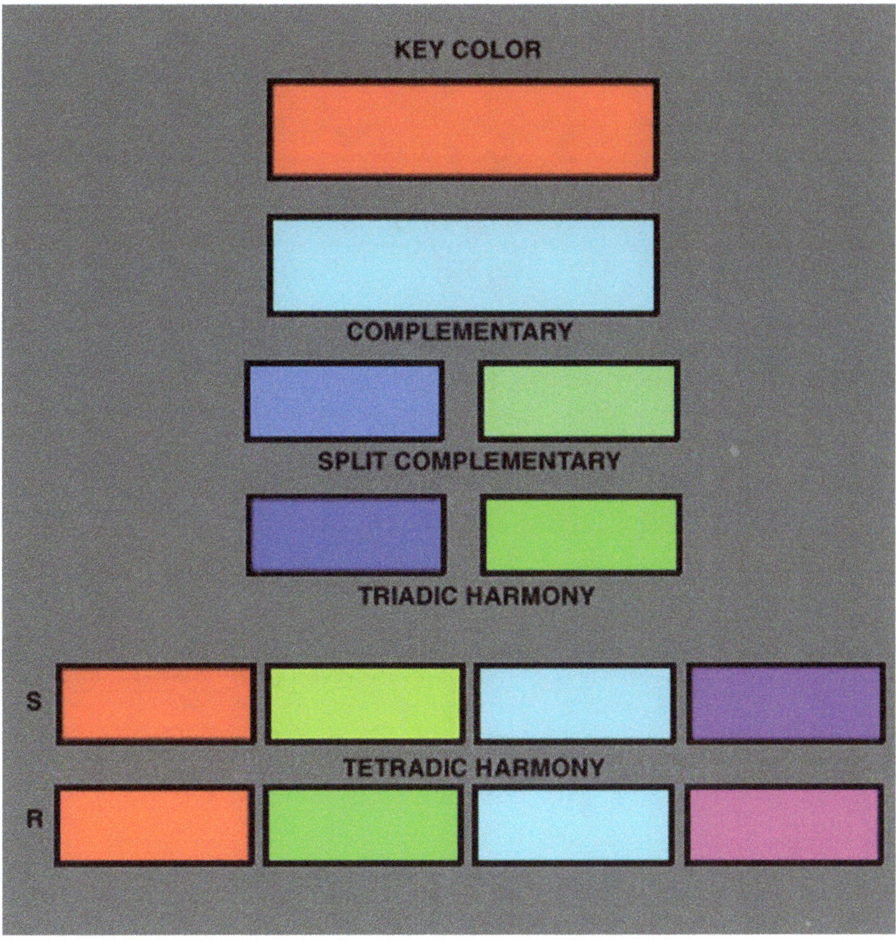

Figure 45 - Computer Color Assistant with Hue Set to H=0

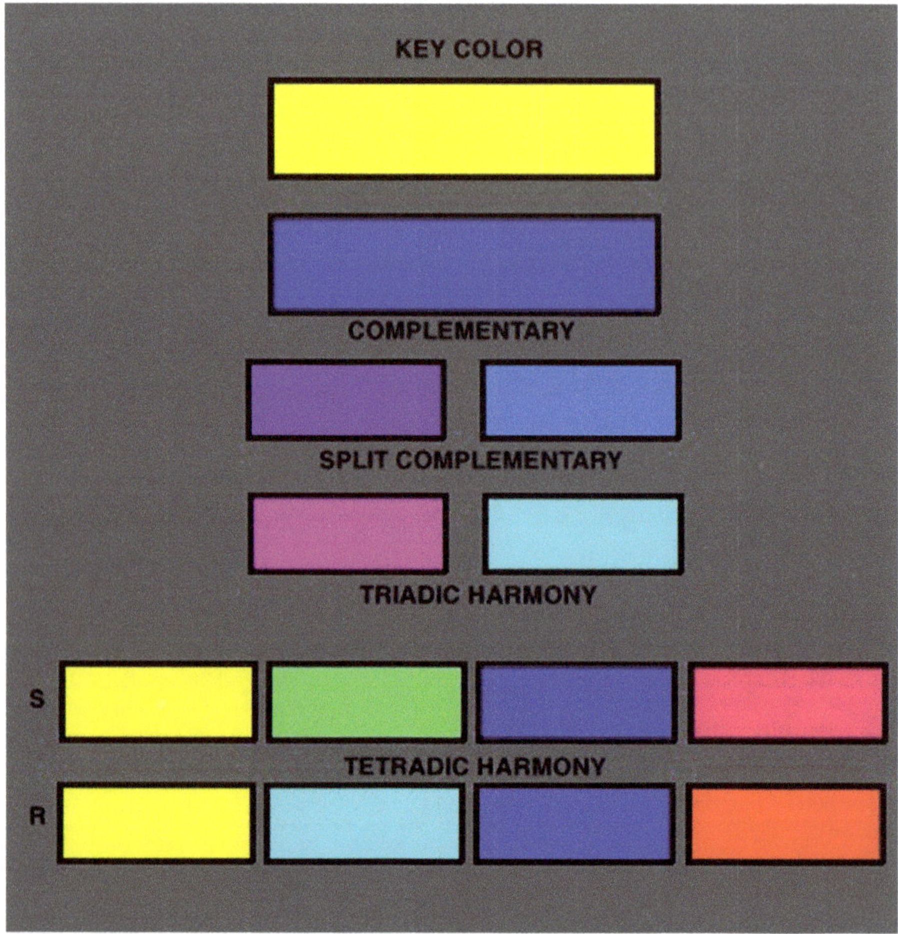

Figure 46 - Computer Color Assistant with Hue Set to H=60

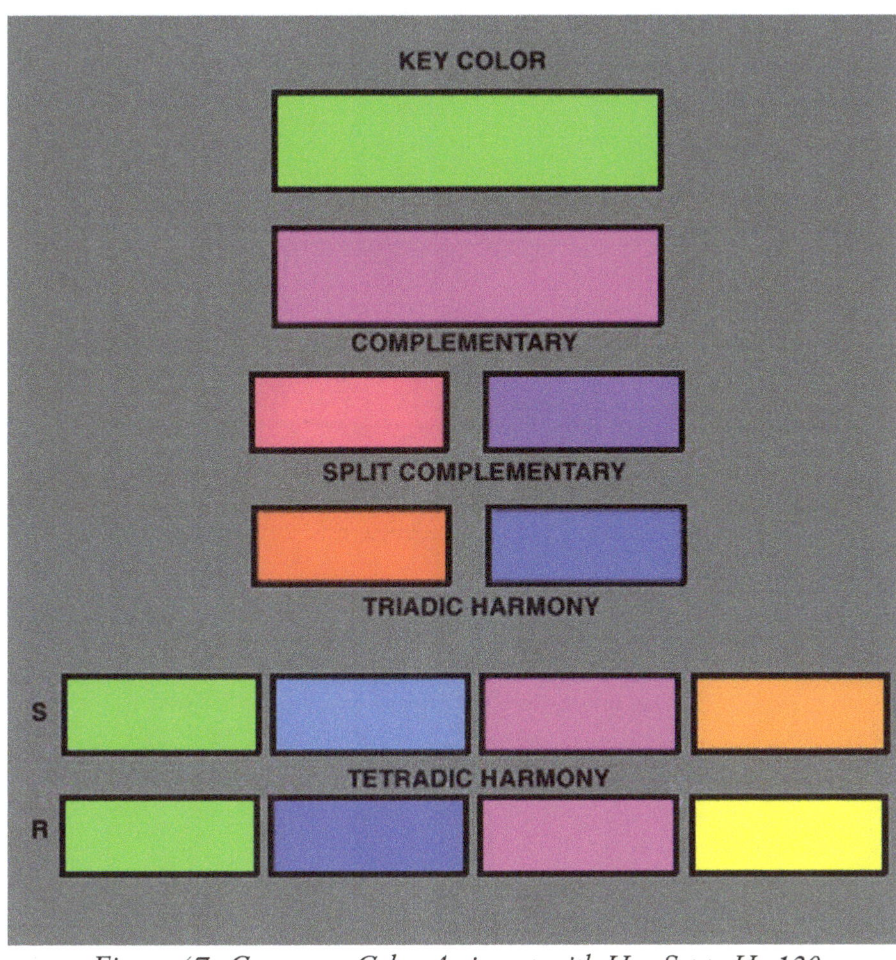

Figure 47 - Computer Color Assistant with Hue Set to H=120

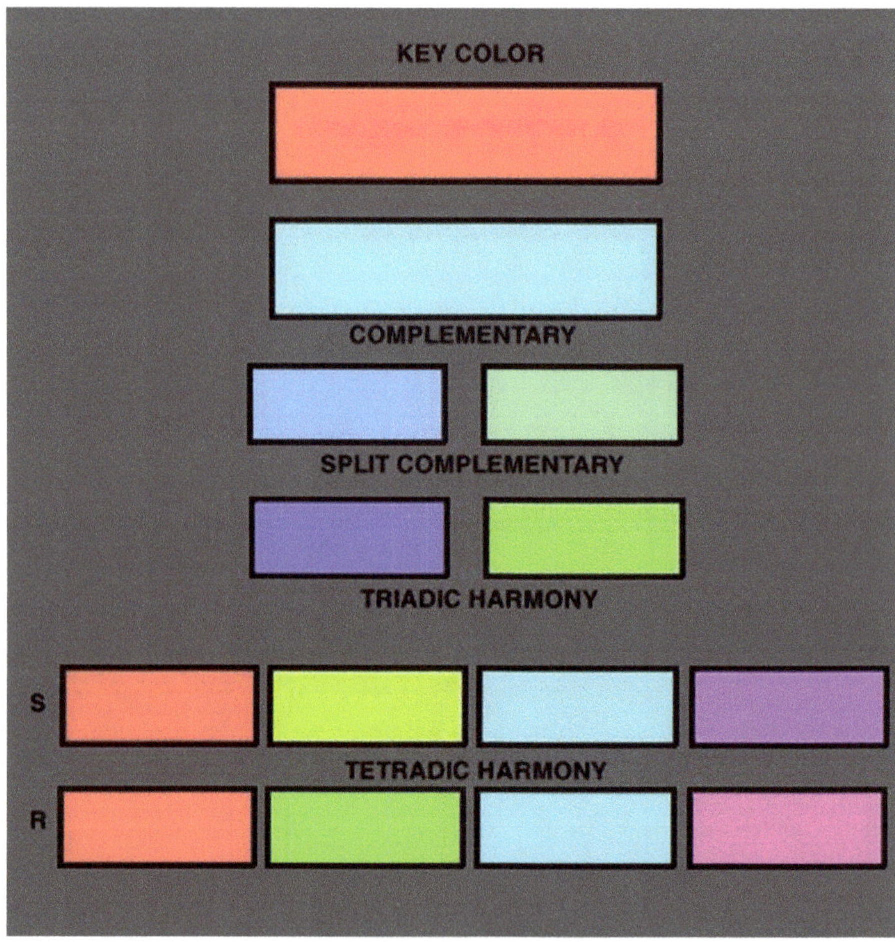

Figure 48 - Computer Color Assistant with Lightness Set to+50

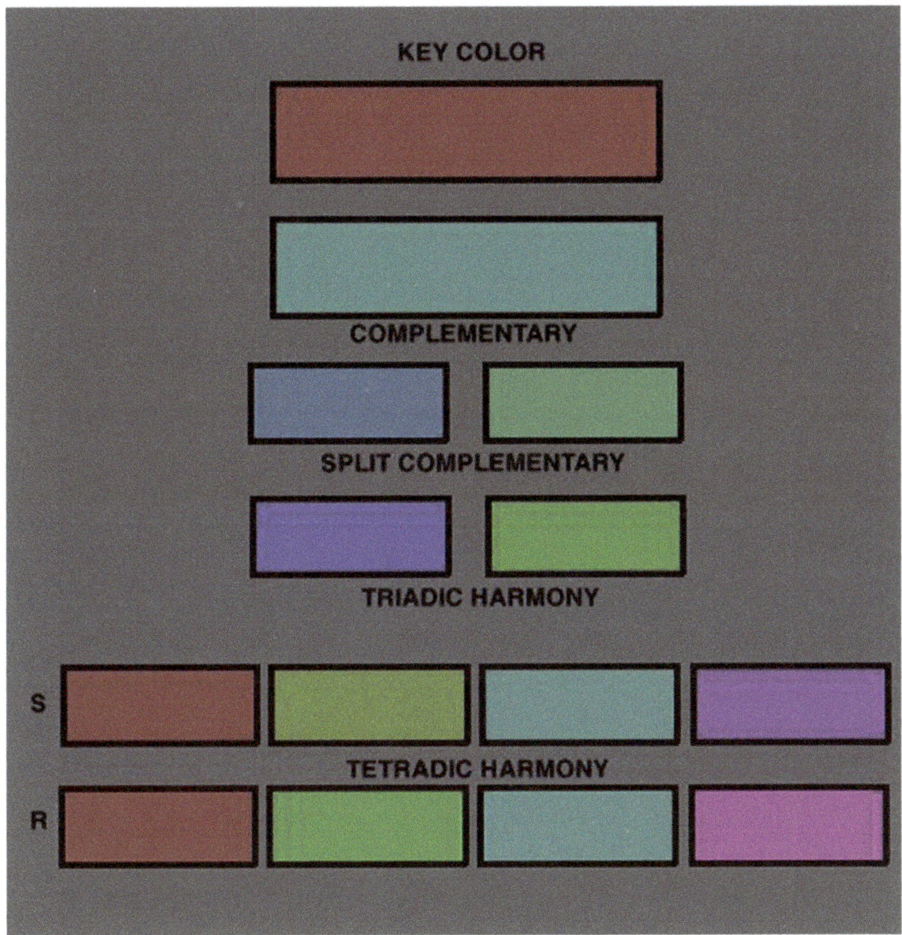

Figure 49 - Computer Color Assistant with Lightness Set to -75

CHROMA SUTRA

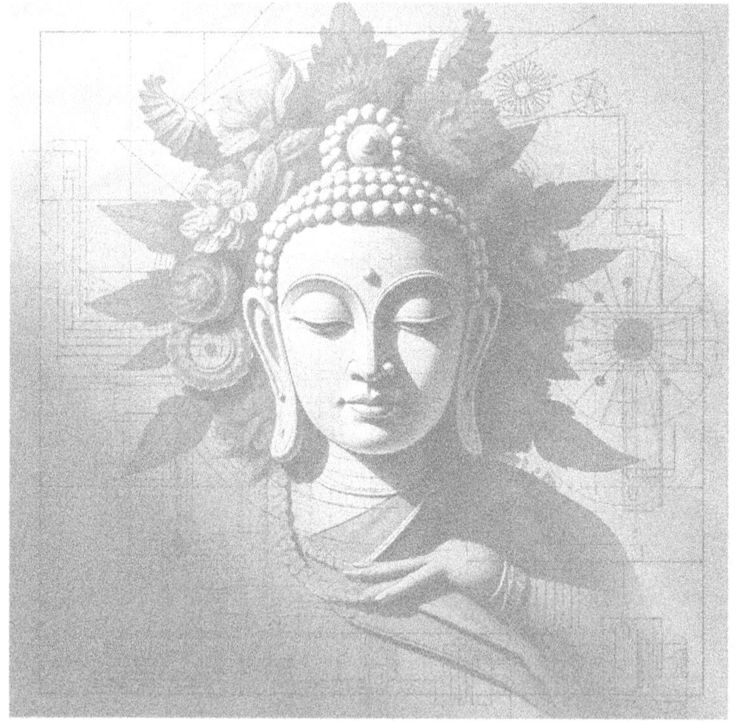

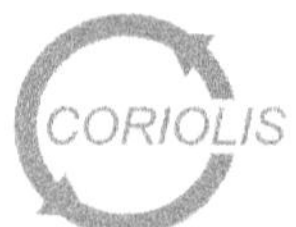

Chapter 11

Some Examples of Color Harmony in Art

Theoretical Analysis of Harmony Using Hue, Complements and the Color Wheel

We can use some of our refined knowledge of color theory to examine existing color harmonies in various historical paintings. Keep in mind there are many ways to analyze a work of art. We can look at contrast, composition or any of the common design elements, but for this study we will look at color harmony, and specifically, the element of color (as opposed to just hue). Remember, complementary colors and complementary hues are two different things. The term "complementary hues" refers only to the hue numbers around the outside of the color wheel. If we add two complementary hues together, we will get black as a result. However, complementary colors will result in a neutral gray somewhere on the value scale. For example, if we have a very light magenta tint, we know the complementary hue is green. But in order get a neutral gray of at least 50% value for visual balance, the relative green color must be much darker than the magenta.

In terms of analysis, to examine complementary color, we simply use the computer. Computers can instantly invert the color data of the image to create a negative or complement. If we want to examine complementary hue, we start with the image and add 180 degrees of hue to it. In the same way, if we wanted to study the values and contrast, we could just discard the color information and make it black and white (gray scale).

Let's start with a completely unknown artist (me), and we'll move along the food chain from there. One of the most powerful tools for analysis of color harmony is the use of complementary data. Put simply, we scan the artwork into the computer, and have the computer then complement the data. In photography, a color negative does exactly the same thing; every color in the artwork becomes its complement. If the two images are placed side-by-side, we can look for similarities and patterns. If we see the same colors in both images, but in different locations, we know the artist was using colors that were precisely complementary. We can also use the computer to measure the actual hue, saturation and value of various colors to try to understand the harmonic relationships that the artist created.

We'll start with an image I painted many years ago, called "Angel with Violin"[1].

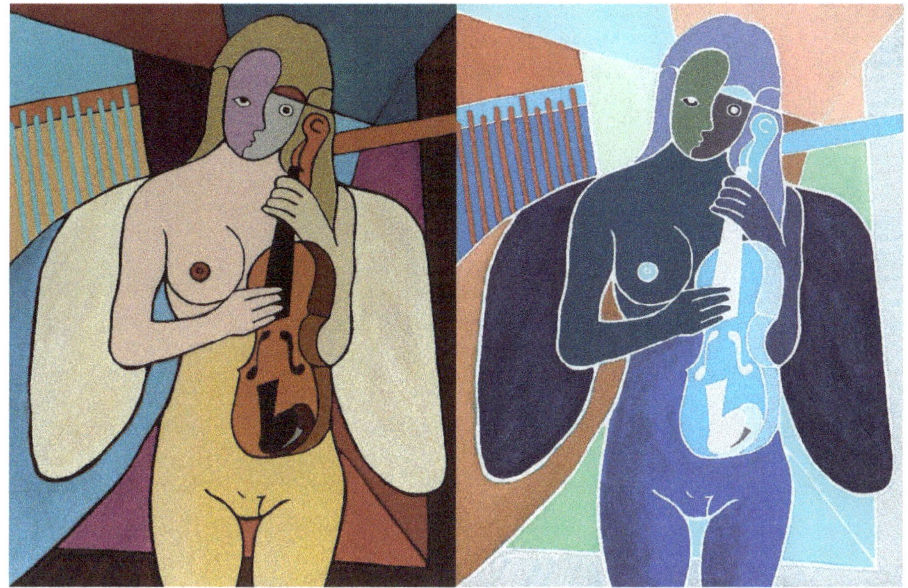

Figure 50 - "Angel with Violin," Walter Holland, 1997, with Inverse

As you can see, I complemented the data and placed them side-by-side. If you study the color wheel diagram and look at any color area on the left side of the image, you will see that the corresponding area on the right side of the image is 180 degrees (or directly across) on a color wheel. Each color in the right side of the image is the exact complement to the one on the left.

---

1. "Angel with Violin," Walter Holland, American, 1997. Courtesy of the Walter Holland Trust.

If we look at the deep red triangle in the upper left corner, it is hue 0. The one on the right is hue 180, and so on, ad infinitum. If we do a fairly quick color harmony analysis, we see that many of the color families are repeated in the complemented image (or "inverse"). For example, the cyan in the background of the painting appears in the violin and several different areas of the inverse on the right. The same is true if we look at the sort of orange bars near the top of the painting and the violin. We see they are repeated in the background, and the rhythmic stripes. You may also notice that the skin tone of the angel is the complement of the large shapes in the upper right of the painting. So, what about the main color harmonies?

This painting uses a tetradic harmony based on colors between cyan and cyan blue (hues 180 - 210) and red to red yellow (hues 0 – 30). In addition, (and this is the part where we learn that rules are just guidelines) the theory suggests that I might sprinkle a bit of hue 285 magenta-magenta-blue for good measure. I did that, and at the last minute I opted to go with a more magenta red hue 320, because I thought it needed the warmth, and just a bit of tension. Close to the theory, but with a human judgment call. So, to summarize, the artist clearly understands color theory and harmony and has an excellent knowledge of complementary colors but also shows a willingness to break rules and take chances with minor deviations from convention when it seems appropriate.

Now, look at “Portrait of a Gentleman,” by Henry Benbridge [2].

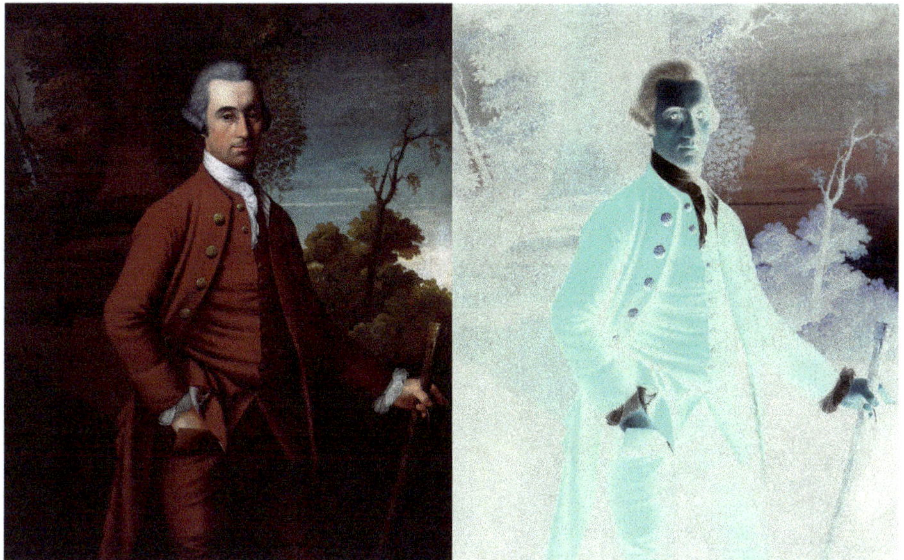

Figure 51 - "Portrait of a Gentleman," Henry Benbridge, 1770-72 with Inverse

This is a simple but effective example of a complementary color scheme based on red (hue 0) and cyan (hue 180). If you notice, the clothing is pure red and the sky is cyan. The background color is also red but with less saturation and lower value. If you look at the inverse image you will see that the background and the clothing are cyan (sky color) and the sky has become the exact color of the background. Benbridge has mixed text-book perfect complementary colors. In addition, the bluish violets of the sky are the exact complements of the yellowish green of the trees. Overall, this painting can be analyzed as a dyadic (two-color) scheme, or

---

2. “Portrait of a Gentleman,” Henry Benbridge, American, 1770-72. Metropolitan Museum of Art, Morris K. Jesup, Maria DeWitt Jesup, and Louis V. Bell Funds, 1969

a tetradic harmony where one pair is predominant. The key to detecting complementary colors is to find the same colors in the left and right images but in different locations.

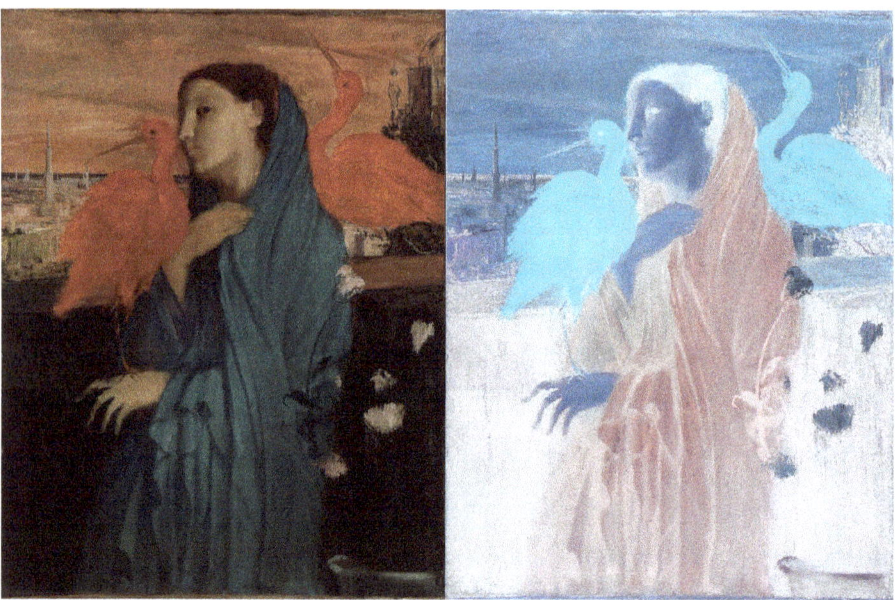

Figure 52 - "Young Woman with Ibis," Edgar Degas, 1857-58, with Inverse

For the next example, let's analyze "Young Woman with Ibis," by Edgar Degas.[3] In this image, you will find precisely the same color harmony scheme that was used in the previous figure (Benbridge). Once again, it is based on red (hue 0) and cyan (hue 180). If you notice, the clothing is deep cyan and the sky is light value red. The background color is also

---

3. "Young Woman with Ibis," Edgar Degas, French, 1857-58. Metropolitan Museum of Art, Gift of Stephen Mazoh and Purchase, Bequest of Gioconda King, by exchange, 2008

red but with a bit less saturation and lighter value, and the birds are pure red. However, this very unusual example works perfectly because of the complementary color scheme. If you look at the inverse image you will see that the background and the birds are now cyan (clothing color) and the clothing has become the exact red color of the sky.

For our next example, we'll use van Gogh's painting "Oleanders."[4] Again, we see that this painting is a classic tetradic harmony. On the warm side of the rectangle, we have anchor points at hue 60, (yellow of the book) and hue 120 (green of the leaves). The background is a combination of the two. The yellow of the book is repeated in the flowers. On the cool side of the rectangle, we have hue 240 (the deep blue of the upper vase) and hue 300 (the light magenta of the flowers). Also notice the magenta / blue (violet) of the shadow is hue 270, halfway between hue 240 and 300, meaning it is a mix of the flower color and the vase color.

So now turn your gaze to the inverse image: We see that the magenta / blue of the table shadow is now the background color. The green of the leaves becomes the light magenta of the oleander flowers. The yellow of the book and flowers becomes the dark blue of the vase. Vincent knew that each one of these colors was the exact color needed for his harmonious scheme. And one more stroke of genius: He included a tiny splash of low value red (hue 0) in the flowers and low value cyan (hue 180) in the vase and the corner of the table. This adds interest with a straight line bisecting our rectangle without disturbing the perfect balance of the tetradic harmony!

---

4. "Oleanders," Vincent van Gogh, Dutch, 1888. Metropolitan Museum of Art, Gift of Mr. and Mrs. John L. Loeb, 1962

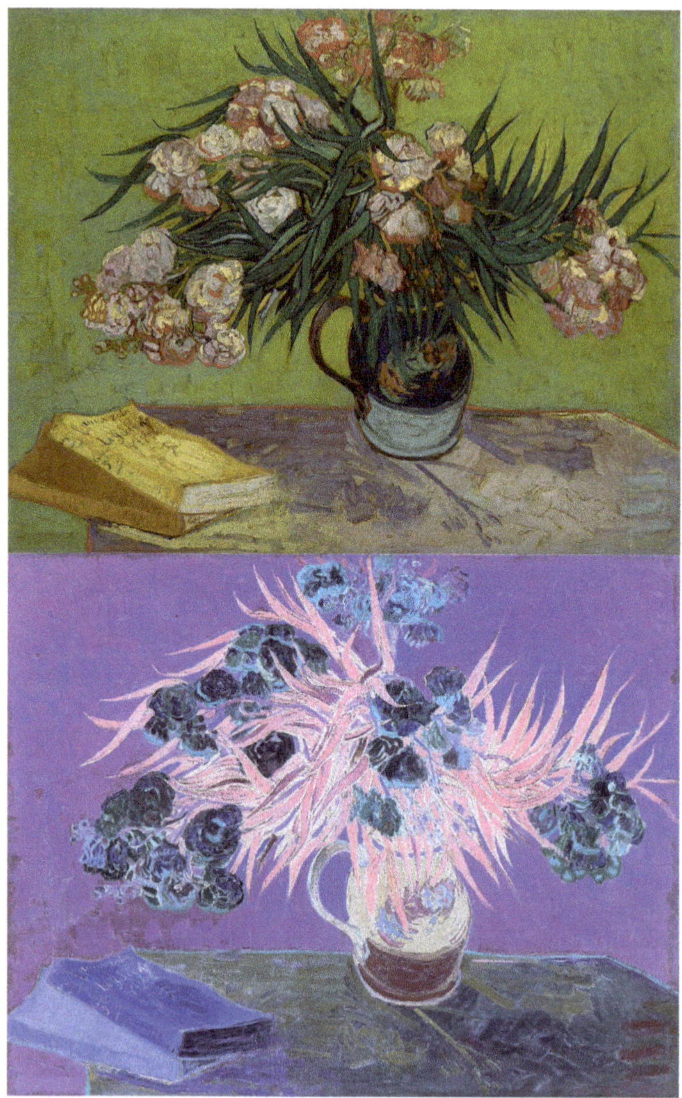

Figure 53 - "Oleanders," Vincent van Gogh, 1888 with Inverse

For our next example we'll study a slightly more complex color scheme by Alfred Sisley, his "View of Marly-Le-Roi."[5] When analyzing a painting with color at this complexity, it is easy to ask: "If he uses every color on the palette, won't we find every color in the inverse image"? The answer to that would likely be yes. However, as complex as this looks it is still a fairly limited palette by the standards of some painters. Let's try to break it down.

This painting can be thought of as another classic tetradic harmony. In fact, this one is strikingly similar to the scheme in the previous van Gogh! Sisley just rotated the colors 30 degrees on the color wheel. On the warm side of the rectangle, we have anchor points at hue 30, (orange of the foliage) and hue 90 (yellow green of the leaves). The ground is a combination of the two. On the cool side of the rectangle, we have hue 210 (the deep cyan blue of the upper sky, the line across the middle and the shape around the base of the trees) and hue 270 (the magenta blue of the tree mounds).

Let's analyze the inverse image: We see that the cyan / blue of the upper sky is now the color of the trees and foliage. The yellow green of the leaves becomes the blue magenta of the tree mounds and city. The orange of the foliage becomes the deep blue of the sky. Once again, the genius splash of low value magenta red (hue 330) in the foreground and low value cyan green (hue 150) in the far right foreground. Again, this adds interest by

---

5. "View of Marly-le-Roi from Coeur-Volant," Alfred Sisley, British, 1876. Metropolitan Museum of Art, Bequest of Miss Adelaide Milton de Groot (1876-1967), 1967

drawing a line bisecting our rectangle without disturbing the balance of the tetradic harmony!

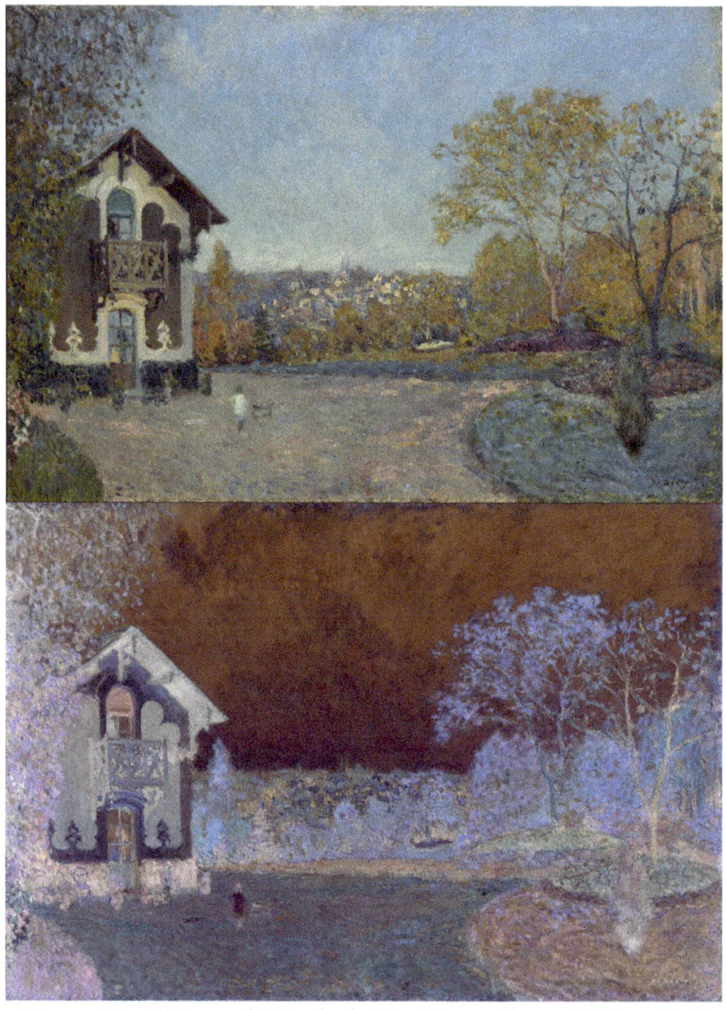

Figure 54 - "View of Marly-le-Roi from Coeur-Volant," Alfred Sisley, 1876, with Inverse

Let's look at van Gogh's "White Cottage Among the Olive Groves."[6] This is a very serene and restful painting, which perfectly demonstrates Vincent's intuitive mastery of color theory. This is once again a very simple tetradic harmony. Meaning, it is based on two pairs of complementary colors. The first pair consists of the blue of the mountains and the yellows of the house and the foreground. These groups of colors are found hovering around hues 60 and 240, (yellows and blues). The second pair consist of the greens of the olive trees and the magentas of the roof and upper left olive tree and foreground tree shadows. These groups of colors are found around hues 120 and 300, (greens and magentas).

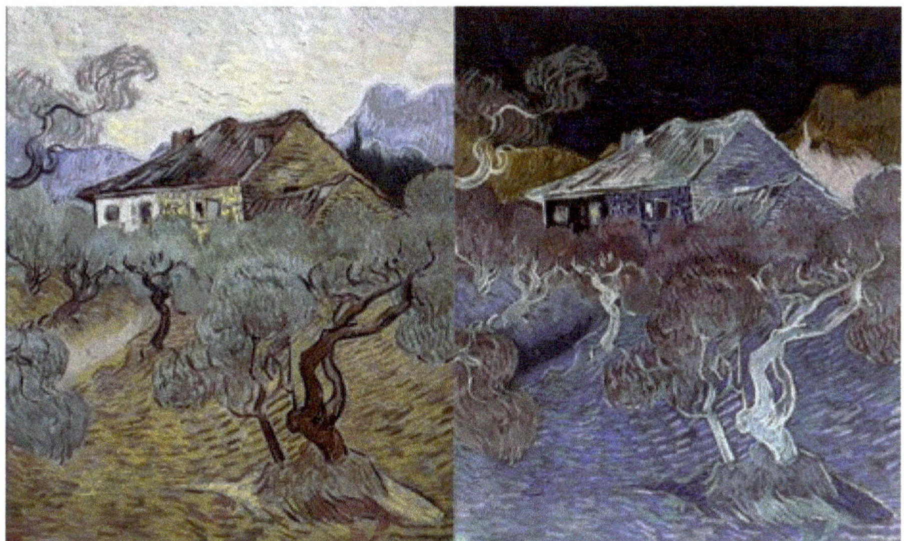

Figure 55 - Vincent Van Gogh, "The White Cottage Among the Olive Groves," 1889 with Inverse

6. "The White Cottage Among the Olive Groves," Vincent van Gogh, Dutch, 1889. Private Collection. Image believed to be in the public domain.

If you look at the right half of the image (all colors complemented) you see that the green branches of the olive trees that had magenta shadows are now magenta with green shadows! They are exact complements! In addition, the yellow foreground and the blue mountains have also switched places. They too are exactly complementary! One may also notice that the dark green foliage behind the house is the exact complementary color of the sky, not just the complementary hue. This is not a coincidence! This demonstrates that Van Gogh had an uncanny, intuitive understanding of the color wheel.

Let's examine Paul Cezanne's "Still Life with Apples and Primroses."[7]

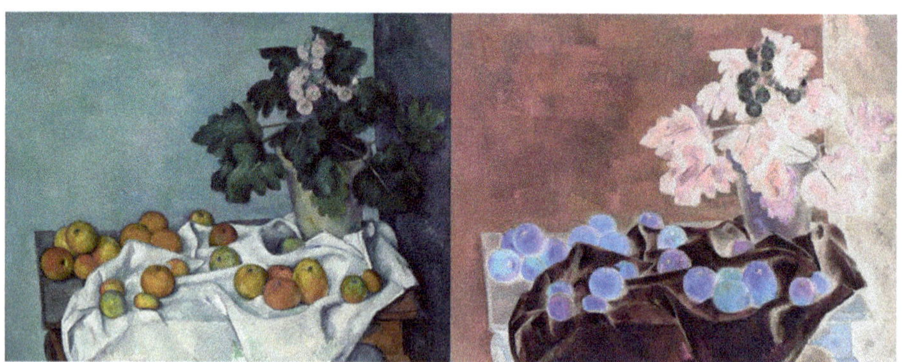

Figure 56 - Paul Cezanne, "Still Life with Apples and a Pot of Primroses," 1890 with Inverse

---

7. "Still Life with Apples and a Pot of Primroses," Paul Cezanne, French, 1890. Metropolitan Museum of Art, Bequest of Sam A. Lewisohn, 1951.

If we study the color of the primroses, we see that they are the complement of the foliage of the leaves. The complement of the yellowest apples can be found in the deep blue of the wall on the right. The blue-green wall color is a lighter variation of the blue-green leaves. Overall, this can be seen as a tetradic harmony, with the main thrust being the cyan blue in the area of Hue 200 and the fruit being red yellow in the range of hue 10-40. There is also another branch of the tetrad that runs from green (hue 130) in the foliage to the magenta in the fruit and primroses (hue 290 – 300). Even though it is a fairly textbook rectangular tetradic harmony, it also contains strong elements of the Red, Yellow, Blue school, which I find a bit retrograde. So now let's take some liberties and play a little game.

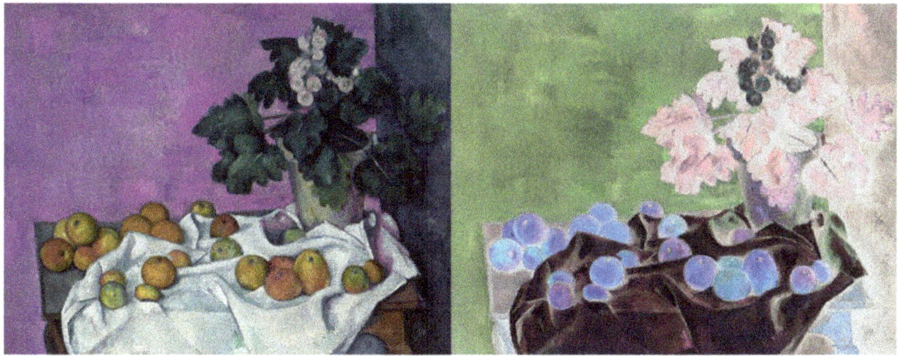

Figure 57 - Paul Cezanne, "Still Life with Apples and a Pot of Primroses," 1890 with Modified Color and Inverse

The only modification I made is to change the wall color in the background from cyan to violet.[8] Without being too judgmental let's look at

8. "Still Life with Apples and a Pot of Primroses," Paul Cezanne, French, 1890. Metropolitan Museum of Art, Bequest of Sam A. Lewisohn, 1951. Color modified for explanatory reasons.

how the analysis has changed. First of all, the foreground and the flowers seem to move forward and not blend so much into the wall. In addition, the wall color is now the complement of the foliage, and in the same family as the primroses. Also, now the colors in the fruit complement both the background and the right half of the wall. I'm not necessarily saying that Cezanne can be improved upon, but it's interesting to speculate when we are analyzing the work. It also shows how one small change to a color harmony can make a substantial difference to the final work.

As long as we're playing color god, let's play one last time with van Gogh. I'll use his well-known "Self Portrait with Bandaged Ear and Pipe" for our next analysis. [9]

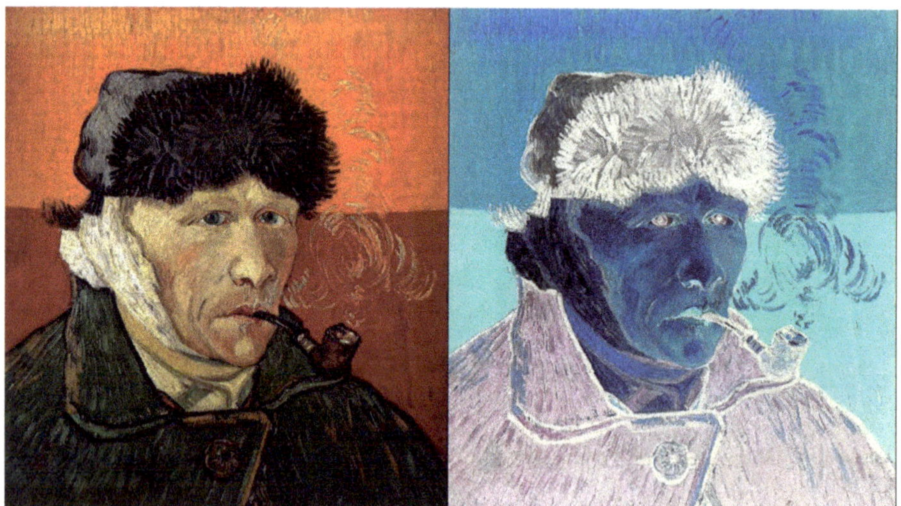

Figure 58 - Vincent van Gogh, Self Portrait with Bandaged Ear and Pipe, 1889 with Inverse

---

9. "Self Portrait with Bandaged Ear and Pipe," Vincent van Gogh, Dutch, 1889. Private Collection. Image believed to be in the public domain.

I consider van Gogh to be a master colorist. His color skills, always apparent, improved intuitively and developed rapidly over time. In my opinion, this is a weak color scheme, for several reasons: It is based on the old Red-Green complementary harmony (which has now been debunked) and the background relies on an analogous dyadic scheme. In addition, the background seems totally unrelated to the foreground. As you can see by the inverted right half of the image, the painting doesn't contain any complementary colors. None of the colors in the left half appear in the right half. The jacket and facial colors seem unrelated for the most part. Using the skin tones as highlights on the jacket was a great idea, but not enough to salvage the color scheme. Don't misunderstand me, this is a very powerful and successful painting, but since we are studying color theory, we must try to understand that isolated element. If you look at the right side of the image, it becomes very clear that the top portion is one color family and the bottom is another, and never the twain shall meet.

I must emphasize, I'm not suggesting van Gogh can be improved upon (and please forgive me Vincent!) but for the sake of analysis let's make one small change to the color harmony. Vincent likes red, so we'll leave that, but we know green is not red's complement so let's make the jacket cyan, which is the complement of red. The only alteration I have made to the image is to change the jacket from green to cyan (okay, maybe the pipe changed color a bit in the process also). So, let's do a new analysis from a color theory point of view.[10]

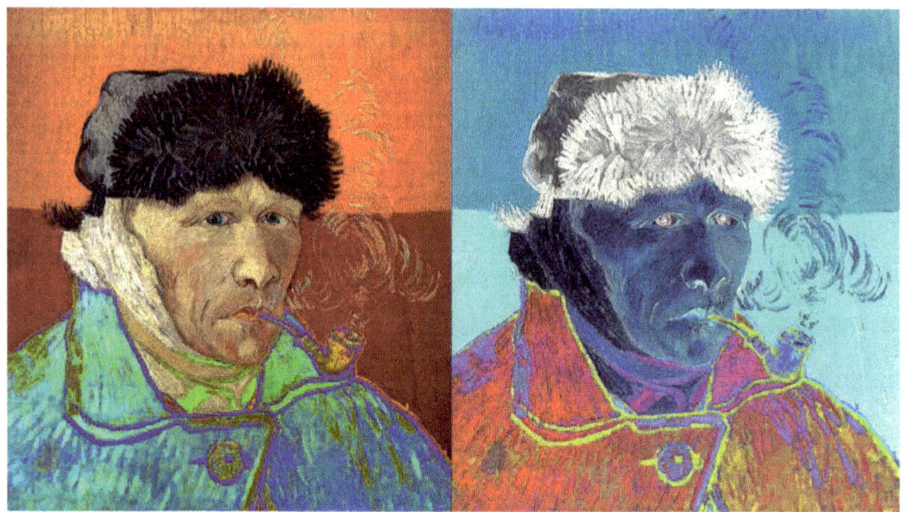

Figure 59 - Vincent Van Gogh, "Self Portrait with Bandaged Ear and Pipe," 1889. Modified Color and Inverse

Now the jacket jumps out of the painting, and in my opinion, the painting comes alive. If we study the complemented image, we see that the colors in the background become the colors in the jacket and vice versa. In addition, the colors in the background and face each have complements to

---

10. "Self Portrait with Bandaged Ear and Pipe," Vincent van Gogh, Dutch, 1889. Private Collection. Image believed to be in the public domain. Color modified for explanatory reasons. (All attempts were diligently made to obtain permission and copyright clearance for these images. If public records indicate that the works are in the public domain, we assumed this to be correct. If this is not correct, we welcome the copyright holders to notify us.)

be found in the painting. There is no real need to make the colors in the jacket as bright as I did. Using less saturated colors and lower values closer to the original painting would have accomplished the same result. The eyes of the viewer are now balanced, and the work seems more contemporary and timeless. By changing one color the overall effect is completely different. Instead of being somber, Vincent looks ready to party. If you brought down the saturation of the jacket, the effect would be that the face would become more prominent, and the somber mood would be restored. By carefully manipulating the colors, any portion of the painting and even the mood can be subtly (or dramatically) altered.

CHROMA SUTRA

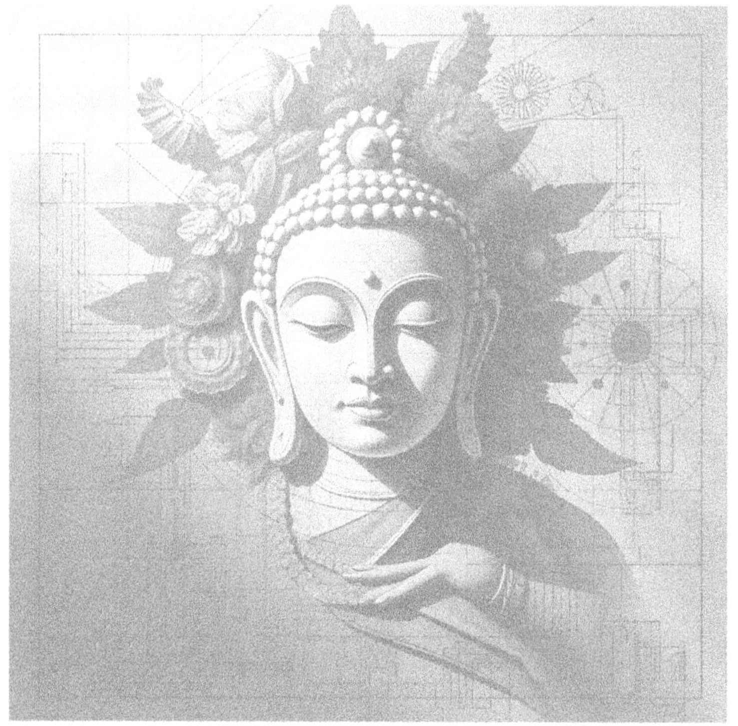

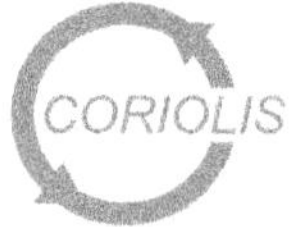

Chapter 12
Apologies to Professor Itten

In 1970, a book was published in the United States that served as a template for the way color would be taught in art schools. This book was called "The Elements of Color" by a Swiss/German art professor named Johannes Itten (Itten, The Elements of Color, 1970). This book was a condensed and simplified version of his major work called "The Art of Color," (Itten, The Art of Color: The Subjective Experience and Objective Rationale of Color, 1974) which Professor Itten had written in 1961. Itten is considered to be one of the greatest teachers of color in modern times and his book is generally regarded as one of the most important and most widely used teaching texts in the field of color for artists. The problem is that much of it is just wrong!

One question that students reading this book will most likely have would be "why in the world would I tackle Johannes Itten, who is considered the god of color, and his textbook, which has served as a virtual bible for artists for the last 60 or more years?" Well, the simple answer is that I think he was mistaken, and I will point out some of things I consider to be fundamental flaws in his thinking.

When I was an art student in college, I learned color from Professor Itten's book, and as an art professor, I had my students study his theory and methods. As I lectured my students and fielded their questions, I became aware of some minor inconsistencies in Itten's work. I must say that there is no better way to have a subject become crystal clear in one's own mind, than to have to explain it in 10 different ways to try to help 10 different students understand the material. The more closely I looked at these inconsistencies, the more I realized that Professor Itten came to what appeared to be invalid conclusions. To make matters even worse, some of the conclusions that I felt were incorrect were premises upon which major portions of his theories were based.

As you might imagine, I was not filled with warmth at the thought of challenging such an accepted and heretofore unquestioned approach to the teaching of color for artists. I was fortunate to be in a unique situation, having a background in both art and science, that I might hear a lecture on color from a physicist, and the same day, attend a lecture on color from an art professor. It was as though each had their own universe of color, and the laws behaved differently for each professor. The physicist said "yellow and blue make black." The artist said "yellow and blue make green." Each of them could prove their view empirically. I struggled with this problem for more than 20 years, and then I decided that since I had this dual background, maybe I could help these two camps sort out their differences. Hence, this book.

If I say Professor Itten was wrong, you deserve to know some specific criticisms. This part may seem a bit disjointed because almost all of his work is interconnected, and much of it is based on early premises. So, if I declare one premise to be incorrect, dominoes begin to fall in many other areas of his work.

One of the main objections I have to Itten's logic is that he states that we should construct the color wheel based on the results he got by mixing paint. The problem is he did not take into account the quality of the paint. If you buy cheap paints, you will find that most color mixes result in brown or gray. This is because they don't contain very much pigment, but do contain fillers, extenders, binders and so on. If you mix blue and yellow, you will get green or even worse, brown. The finest pigments available to Itten (and for the last 300 years) weren't much better, and I believe this colored his results (if you'll pardon the wordplay). It is only in recent years that we have pigments of sufficient quality to render color theory usable. Itten was correct to suggest afterimages as a way to locate colors on the color wheel. However, his experiments were poorly constructed, and his results verified his incorrect color wheel. So, what would my approach to the problem be? I would start with the additive theory of light. This is color theory in its purest form, since it reflects the way the eye works and human perception.

We know that the receptors in the eye are sensitive to: red, green and blue and therefore those must be the primary colors, since all colors we can perceive can be made from those three primaries. Because as artists we are working with pigments (and therefore reflected light) we complement the data, and the primary colors become cyan, magenta and yellow. Remember that for pigments we complement (invert the data for) the primaries: magenta is (-green), cyan is (-red) and yellow is (-blue). If we build a color wheel around this data, we find that Itten has most of his colors in the wrong position. One other thing of note is that even though we have known this to be true for some time, (this data was well known at Itten's time) the color wheels at most art stores, libraries and most web based learning sites are still incorrect. If you are paying down student loans for an expensive art education, you were very likely taught the wrong color wheel! Additionally, we now have pigments that are of sufficient quality to allow us to mix blue and yellow and get black, as the analytic approach predicts. In fact, these days I can mix red and cyan, magenta and green or any other set of complements and still get black.

Many of Itten's assumptions are based on his vision of a color wheel, which has most of the colors placed incorrectly. Itten also bases many assumptions on his experiments with color afterimages, which were also incorrect but were used to develop the wheel. We have addressed these problems and can see that it leads to even more erroneous conclusions, the further one carries the logic.

In the section on physics, Itten describes Newton's experiments with a prism and describes the relationships of complementary colors. However, in most cases he describes the incorrect result. As one example, he says if we isolate green from the spectrum and recombine the remaining colors, the result will be red. The actual result is magenta, which is a very different color. This is fascinating, because there is no pure magenta wavelength in the spectrum. However, after we combine the component colors and subtract green, the result is magenta! This should have been a red flag to investigate further. These incorrect results just happen to be the incorrect complements he uses in his theories about color wheels, complementary colors, color harmonies and afterimages. Since his entire foundation for the majority of the book is flawed, it requires the reader to take the information with a grain of salt, and at very least adjust his theories to fit with the corrected color wheel.

So back to our main question: how do you reconcile the difference between art and physics? Another way of asking might be: Why are the answers in art so different from the answers in physics? A large portion of the problem manifests itself because of the cheap paint we use. In the study of light, we know the additive primary colors are red, green, and blue. It should logically follow that with pigments, which typically are subtractive components, (that is, they work according to the laws of subtraction), the primary colors should be magenta, yellow, and cyan. Another way to say this is that pigments selectively remove red, green and blue light that otherwise would have reached our eyes. If then, you make a color wheel based on the subtractive primaries, red, yellow, and blue, which are thought to be the artist's primaries, it turns out to be incorrect. The fundamental problem with "Artist's Primaries" is that red and blue are both secondaries in the subtractive system. They are only primaries in the additive system, and that only works for light! Therefore, they cannot be primary colors for mixing paint!

Another huge issue is, according to the laws of subtraction, yellow and blue, when mixed, should yield black. And of course, they rarely do. Artists are used to seeing green, or brownish green as results. These are just a few of the historical problems of reconciling art and physics. So, my investigation began by trying to figure out why mixing yellow and blue frequently yields green. I've come up with some interesting findings. First, mixing yellow and blue violates one of the first rules of subtractive pigment mixing and that is the resultant color should always be darker than the two original colors. In practical experience, when you mix yellow with anything the resulting color is often lighter. This is a significant problem, and the answer is counter-intuitive. I thought about this for a long time, in fact, many years. I couldn't come up with the answer until I started looking at spectral reflectance curves of various pigments. I realized that what one would expect is that each pigment should act like a bandpass filter, reflecting only wavelengths right around the center frequency of the that pigment. Well, in fact this is not what happens at all. When you look at spectral reflectance curves of most of the common artist's colors, you find that blue and green work essentially the way one would expect them to work. However, red is much more like a low-pass filter in the sense that instead of reflecting just one narrow band right around its center frequency, it reflects red and everything below red. Orange is the same way. Orange reflects everything up to orange, including red. Yellow is worse than any of them. Yellow also works like a sort of a low-pass filter in that it reflects everything from green down. Now this shelving effect causes a serious problem because you're expecting a pigment that's only reflecting yellow and in fact, you're getting green and red and everything in between. Now, when green and red mix in the eye, you see yellow anyway, so it's not a problem in that sense. What causes the problem is that since you have all these other colors being reflected, that is to say, almost everything except blue, you get a pigment that behaves nearly the same way that white does. You essentially increase the amount of light that reaches your eye. And that's why when you mix colors with some yellows, everything ends up lighter. This statement refers to cheaper pigments. When you follow my instructions using Maimeri paint, mixing yellow and blue does make black and it is indeed darker, after adding yellow. The reason for this is that the eye is sensitive to red, green and blue light. The blue pigment absorbs everything else but reflects blue light. Adding the yellow pigment now absorbs all of the blue light and since no light reaches our eye, our brain tells us the pigment is black.[1]

One additional complication to this problem is that there is no pure magenta wavelength in the spectrum of white light. And magenta is obviously a fairly important component if we're expecting to use the rules of subtraction. When you look at the spectral reflectance curves of a magenta pigment, what you see are reflectance peaks in the red end and in the blue and violet end. These mix in the eye to fool you into seeing magenta. Oh yes, back to Itten. I'm reading through the introduction to Itten's book, and I'll comment on some of the places where I feel that he may have gone a little bit astray.

Itten refers to master colorists and names a few people. My color wheel is very different from Itten's so I would consider some of his master colorists that based their work on incorrect color wheels to be, well, incorrect. I do

---

1. Remember Holland's Law of Absorption.

consider Van Gogh to be a master colorist. But if I look at a complete book of his paintings, I can find paintings that he had done early in his career that utilize the textbook (that is, incorrect) color theory, as it was taught at the time. I think that produced some of his weaker paintings. I can also find some of his most powerful works where the color harmonies are based entirely and almost exactly to the color wheel that I'm proposing. I believe at some point Van Gogh worked out or discovered or knew intuitively how these color relationships are pleasing and produced his best work.

In reality there are a large number of different color issues and Itten studied many of the different types. I cannot find fault with the way that he looks at many of them. My main goal is to write a book that will explain the physics of color in a way that artists can understand it, and in a way that artists can apply it in a practical sense. In order that they are able to understand color harmonies, and they know intuitively how to mix colors to come up with successful, pleasing, aesthetic schemes. It looks like the real serious work and the rationale for color systems started about the beginning of the 19th century. There was a work published by Goethe in 1810, "Theory of Colours" or Zur Farbenlehre (Goethe, 1810), and in 1839 Chevreul published "De la Loi du Contraste Simultané des Couleurs" (Chevreul, 1839).

It's fascinating that Itten is talking about Mondrian and what an important contribution he made by using pure yellow, red, and blue to construct paintings whose form and color coincide in the effect of static equilibrium,[2] (which is not strictly technically correct). But the thing that I find interesting is it doesn't matter if you're talking about light or pigment. The primary colors that your eye is looking for are red, green and blue.

---

2. Itten, "Elements of Color" Page 12.

You'd still be getting those particular wavelengths to your eye, in close to theoretically pleasing amounts.

Itten bases much of his color theory on the concept of afterimages, saying that this phenomenon is an important part of the physiological aspect of color. Well, when I performed the basic afterimage test based on the examples in his book, I got answers entirely different than he did and mine correspond to the color wheel that I'm proposing. I guess there's some possibility that he was so convinced that his theory was correct that even when he did after- image tests, he got answers that confirmed his theory, whether they were entirely accurate or not. Itten has a great quote that might serve as an introduction to my book, (if I didn't feel too guilty about attacking his work to use it): "Only those who love color are admitted to its beauty and immanent presence. It affords utility to all but unveils its deeper mysteries only to its devotees."[3]

At this point in the introduction,[4] Itten is writing about how he defines colors. I think I'll probably start taking exception with him right there at the beginning. He talks about the quality of a color, and he defines that as its location around the outside of the color circle. I would like to refer to that as hue. When he talks about the degree of lightness or darkness of a color, he calls this quantity or brilliance. He also sometimes refers to it as a tonal gradation. I think I will refer to that as value. And in terms of how do you define how much a color is grayed down, I'm going to refer to that as saturation.

Itten talks about the idea that you can split white light into the various colors, and when you subtract one, you get its complement, which should

---

3. Itten, "Elements of Color" Page 13.

4. The Elements of Color, Johannes Itten, Introduction

be a fairly well-known, verifiable piece of physics. Except when he starts talking about the colors that result when you recombine them. He goes back to his own color wheel and I suspect that if you really investigate that experiment and repeat it, you'll find that the resulting colors actually match my color wheel. Itten claims that if you subtract green from the spectrum and you mix the remaining colors which are red, orange, yellow, blue and violet, the combined color will be red. However, my guess is if you mix so many different colors of light together, you're going to get a result that is very, very light, and it will most likely be magenta, which is the color that I claim should be the opposite on the color wheel, and the complementary color. I believe he saw the result as red, because he may not have even known of the existence of magenta. After all, it isn't in the spectrum, and perceptual theory wasn't very well developed at that time.

Itten spends a lot of time talking about what he calls color effect. This is the interaction of colors in relation to other colors, when placed in proximity. Now, I'm primarily going to concern myself with what he calls color agent, the pigments themselves, and that is trying to look at the colors and their harmonic relationships in the absolute sense. He talks about how colors are altered by their proximity to other colors. I think he's done a fabulous job of that, and I'm going to refer any of those types of problems to his work. As I read through his first chapter, I'm beginning to think that the problems he runs into later are largely because of the semantic looseness or semantic sloppiness that he uses (for example, calling Magenta "Red").

As I mentioned earlier, he talks about subtracting green out of the total spectrum and ending up with red. My guess is he was actually ending up with magenta. And he was calling it red. And now when Itten refers to complementary colors, and talking about them containing all the primaries, my head explodes. He says that when you mix blue and orange you get a pleasing combination because the result is blue plus (yellow and red). My issue is that we already know blue and red are not primaries in the subtractive system. What was really happening is that when you mix yellow (not orange) and blue, the eye gets blue light from the blue and red and green light from the yellow, therefore all three primaries. And it follows that blue and yellow are complements, not blue and orange. Is it really a mystery that artists are confused by this complete confusion?

Itten says that two or more colors are mutually harmonious if their mixture yields neutral gray. I would say he is absolutely correct, as long as we realize that black and white and all values in between are also neutral. The problem is that at Itten's time the quality of the pigments were so bad that most color mixes were likely to result in grays or browns.

My basic premise is going to be: forget about mixing results, since most pigments are of low quality and do not follow true rules of subtraction. I believe you should base all your laws of color on additive rules because they will teach you the truth about the way light and the eye behave. Then you need to understand the limitations of pigments. If you understand the basic principles of color addition and the limitations of pigments, you will be able to create a much broader range of colors, and you'll understand how color harmonies and relationships work.

It may turn out that thinking in terms of complementary pairs, which is the way Itten thought, isn't such a bad idea, so long as you have the correct pairs, which he didn't. I believe it's more accurate and useful to think in terms of the three primaries and to analyze every color in relation to those primaries. As an example, you might say, I'm looking at blue and I want to know how it is made up in terms of magenta, cyan and yellow. In other words, is this blue too cyan? Is it too yellow? Is it too magenta? I believe any color can be analyzed in terms of the three primaries more accurately than it can be based on complementary pairs.

Itten also talks about the fact that harmonious colors result as some kind of regular orderly harmonic relationship, in the same way that musical notes have mathematical relationships. So maybe someday, I can look at the spectrum and find out if any harmonic relationships actually exist. I agree with Itten that the foundation of any aesthetic color theory is the color circle and that that should determine the classification of colors and harmonies. I also agree with Itten that it is important to base color theory on the laws of afterimage. However, I think it's extremely important that we truly analyze afterimage. And we may find that this new color wheel that I'm proposing, which encompasses the laws of addition and subtraction, may work out to be a much sounder and more rewarding approach. As an added bonus, afterimages just confirm the additive and subtractive information we have established as reliable.

Now we're getting to the point where Itten says the color artist must work with pigments, and therefore, his color classification must be constructed in terms of mixing of pigments. That is to say, diametrically opposed colors must be complementary, mixing to yield gray. This I think is the most fundamental premise of Itten's that I disagree with. His conclusions are wrong, because they don't consider the quality of the paint. If you buy cheap paint, all color mixes will result in brown or gray. Merely switching to any different brand is likely to alter your results. In fact, he goes on to say that in his color circle blue stands opposite to an orange because of the fact that when you mix those two colors you get gray. This may be true in some cases, but hardly a scientific basis for a color theory! And, Itten has said that in (German physicist) Wilhelm Ostwald's color circle (Ostwald, 1942), blue stands opposite to yellow, a pigmentary mixture yielding green (which Itten thought couldn't possibly be right). Except Ostwald, as it turns out, was correct and with good paint, yellow and blue do make black. And yes, mixing blue and yellow sometimes does yield green, but it's because of the extreme limitation of the yellow pigment. I think it's more important for an artist to understand the correct theory than to be able to mix some arbitrary color combinations and always get gray, as claimed by Itten. And, on top of that, Professor Itten, mixing pure complementary hues should yield black, not gray! (See Complementary Hue vs. Complementary Color)

As I have said previously, until I was blue in the face, I think "The Elements of Color" is a marvelous work, and that all artists should read it, but it is critical for one to mine the useful information and disregard the portion that has been proven to be obsolete. To Professor Itten: I apologize profusely for having to correct your mostly fabulous work and please know that I was only attempting (with my corrections), to guide students back onto the path to success.

As I always say, when it comes to color, there is no such thing as black and white.

Appendix - Holland's Laws of Color Theory for Artists

Confirmation of Holland's Laws of Color Theory for Artists: Elucidation of the Process, Underlying Principles and Conclusions.

Walter Holland, Adjunct Professor of Art

Abstract

In the book *Chroma Sutra – The Holland Lectures on Color Theory for Artists*[1] , I attempt to introduce a new, more accurate and comprehensive version of color theory for artists. This new approach aims to correct hundreds of years of misinformation and flawed data that has been built upon and propagated throughout the artistic and academic communities. Interestingly, the information that has been taught to scientists during the same time period has been accurate and empirically verifiable, which has led to a schism between the two disciplines. My original vision was to present the information in a way that was accessible to artists while maintaining scientific accuracy. It was necessary to leave out much of the

1. *Walter G. Holland Chroma Sutra – The Holland Lectures on Color Theory for Artists, (Lake Elsinore, CA:* Coriolis, 2024).

research in order to meet this goal. Nonetheless, this paper attempts to "show the work" that lead to the recognition of anomalies and the resulting processes of research and conclusions reached, while discussing how and why the Holland Model of Color Theory for Artists was developed, and to test its veracity.

Introduction

The textbook, *Chroma Sutra – The Holland Lectures on Color Theory for Artists*[2] is the culmination of nearly 50 years of study of color and more than 40 years of lecturing on the topic. The purpose of this paper is to "show the work" as it was done; to articulate the theoretical framework, and to show how the various laws and relationships were derived and refined.

Initially, I observed that most artists, (myself included) had tremendous difficulty learning and implementing color theory. The four most frequent causes of consternation were: 1) determining what constitutes the primary colors; 2) understanding theoretical harmonic relationships; 3) use of low-quality pigments; and 4) mixing paint colors reliably and repeatably. I theorized that there must be something wrong with the manner in which color theory is taught in academia, if the majority of its graduates continue to have the same issues they had upon entering art education programs. As it turns out, a large portion of what is being taught is confusing and incorrect. Some of the premises upon which modern color theory is built are to this day being taught incorrectly, causing subsequent reasoning to be faulty with confounding and disappointing results.

The Determination of Primary Colors

---

2. Ibid.

The Problem:

Most teachers and students believe that red, yellow and blue are the primary colors. This is a fallacy. In fact, in the subtractive color domain used for paint mixing, red and blue are secondary colors. This has historically been the root of numerous failings.[3]

The Research:

How do we determine what the primary colors are? If we look at human perceptual models of color, we know there are three types of receptors for color information. These are the cones, located at the back of the retina in an area known as the fovea. These cones are designated as Long, Medium and Short (sensitive to Red, Green and Blue wavelengths of light).[4] There is considerable spectral overlap[5] in the operational ranges of the cone types, but it is these three wavelengths: red, green and blue that allow us to see all of the colors in the rainbow.

---

3. Johannes Itten *The Elements of Color*. (New York: Van Nostrand Reinhold, 1970). In this landmark book Itten makes multiple references to the primary colors of red, yellow and blue and praises Mondrian for elevating their use.

4. Vincent A. Billock, Gerald A. Gleason and Brian H. Tsou Perception of forbidden colors in retinally stabilized equiluminant images: an indication of softwired cortical color opponency? 2001 J. Opt. Soc. Am. Vol. 18 No. 10 Oct 2001

5. Ibid.

[6]

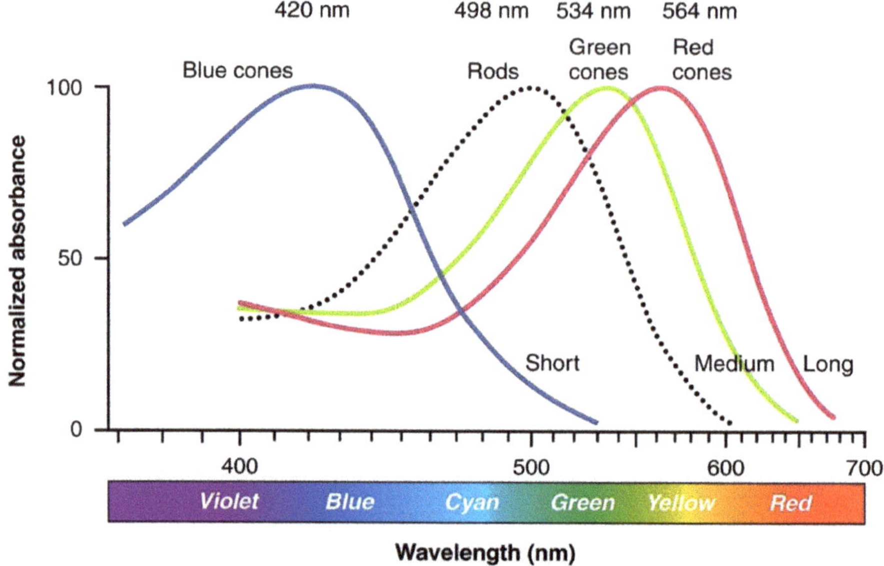

Fig. 1. Human Cone Cell Spectral Response

The fact that all visible colors can be generated by the proportional combination of these three colors, allows us to determine that these must therefore be the primary colors. A modern LED television or computer monitor only emits these three wavelengths, yet when added together, we perceive the entire spectrum of colors. Therefore, we call these (red, green and blue) the additive primary colors.

In order to mix paint or other pigments, however, we need to view the theory a bit differently. Paint works by subtracting out (absorbing) the majority of the light that strikes it and selectively reflecting the remaining wavelengths. There is no need, however, to discover different primary colors. Since mixing paint is a subtractive process, we simply need to use

---

6. By OpenStax College - Anatomy & Physiology, Connexions Web site. http://cnx.org/content/col11496/1.6/, Jun 19, 2013., CC BY 3.0, https://commons.wikimedia.org/w/index.php?curid=30148003

the mathematical complements of the additive primaries. Red becomes (-cyan), green becomes (-magenta) and blue becomes (-yellow). This fact can be proven with afterimage testing, along with many other confirmational methods. Each of these complements is the additive primary plus 180 degrees of hue on the standardized composite color wheel. One of the additional mathematical symmetries is that all of the subtractive primary colors are secondary colors in the additive system, and vice versa. A common example of this inverted data relationship is a color photographic film negative; anything red in the photo will appear as cyan on the negative (and in fact another verification of our complementary colors and their placement on the color wheel).[7]

Historically there has been another method traditionally used to verify the primary colors and their mathematical complements; that is by using "afterimages."[8] This is in fact the method that Johannes Itten used to develop his color theory, and the traditional color wheel. Unfortunately, he reached incorrect conclusions with both, and the confusion has persisted, much like the afterimages.[9]

If one stares at a green sample and then stares at a blank white page, you will see a magenta afterimage. Not in fact red as proposed by Itten. Staring at a blue sample will produce a yellow afterimage. Staring at a red sample

---

7. , Walter G. Holland 1985, Proposed. Verified and named 2023, Holland Standardized Composite Color Wheel. See Fig. 3 above.

8. See note 3 above. See also after-images tests (Figures 5-7) in illustration section.

9. See note 3 above. Itten was incorrect, page 19. Verify for yourself with included tests, (Figures 5-7).

will produce a cyan afterimage. None of these results agree with Itten's results, yet they have a profound effect on the accuracy of color theory, and the subsequent development of the color wheel.

One of the major outcomes of correcting the results from afterimage testing is that we have verified the correct complementary colors for the additive primaries, and by definition, conversely for the subtractive primaries. It is important to keep in mind that the two domains contain the same information, just complemented. The second outcome is that we now suspect that the afterimage is generated not as a response to stimulation of particular receptor, but in fact a response self-generated by the pair of receptors not being stimulated. The addition of these two remaining (unused) primary receptors in fact creates the secondary color perception which is the complement of the first receptor. This bolsters the idea that the system can create its own information by way of a servo feedback mechanism. (For details, see the section on the Holland "Black Box" model of Color Perception).

The Solution:

When mixing light in the additive domain (such as theater lighting or viewing computer monitors) we use the additive primary colors of red, green and blue. When mixing paint or pigments in the subtractive domain, we use the subtractive primaries of magenta, cyan and yellow. All possible colors can be created in either the additive or subtractive domain by using the appropriate primary colors and mixing them in the proper proportions.

The resulting symmetry and beauty of having the colors placed correctly on the wheel, is that the wheel can be used to solve color problems in either the additive or subtractive domain. The subtractive domain is simply the mathematical complement of the additive domain. For those not accustomed to Boolean Logic, simply add 180 degrees of hue (or look directly across the wheel) to convert between the additive and subtractive domains.

The Determination of Colors and Placement on the Color Wheel

The Problem:

Virtually all the color wheels used in teaching color theory contain major errors or are completely incorrect. This leads to errors in teaching color harmony, and paint mixing nightmares. For example, how does one teach that colors 180 degrees opposite from each other on the wheel are complements, when all of the colors are in the wrong places? Example: traditional color wheels have red and green opposite each other, yet red and green are certainly not complements. This is shoddy science and leads to muddy results.[10]

The Research:

In practice, 12 appears to be an optimal number of colors for artists to use as a color wheel reference. Most people can easily visualize 12 colors and remember them. Finer divisions can be extrapolated with ease. More color divisions than this becomes cumbersome and redundant[11] . By using

---

10. Figure 2. is an image of a traditional color wheel typical of the ones sold commercially. This configuration is no longer considered valid.

11. I am referring to artists here. In industry it is common to have many more colors in a given system in order to have increased specificity. This can be seen in the Pantone Matching System, RAL, Munsell, and many other systems.

an even number, we also ensure that complementary colors remain 180 degrees apart on the wheel.

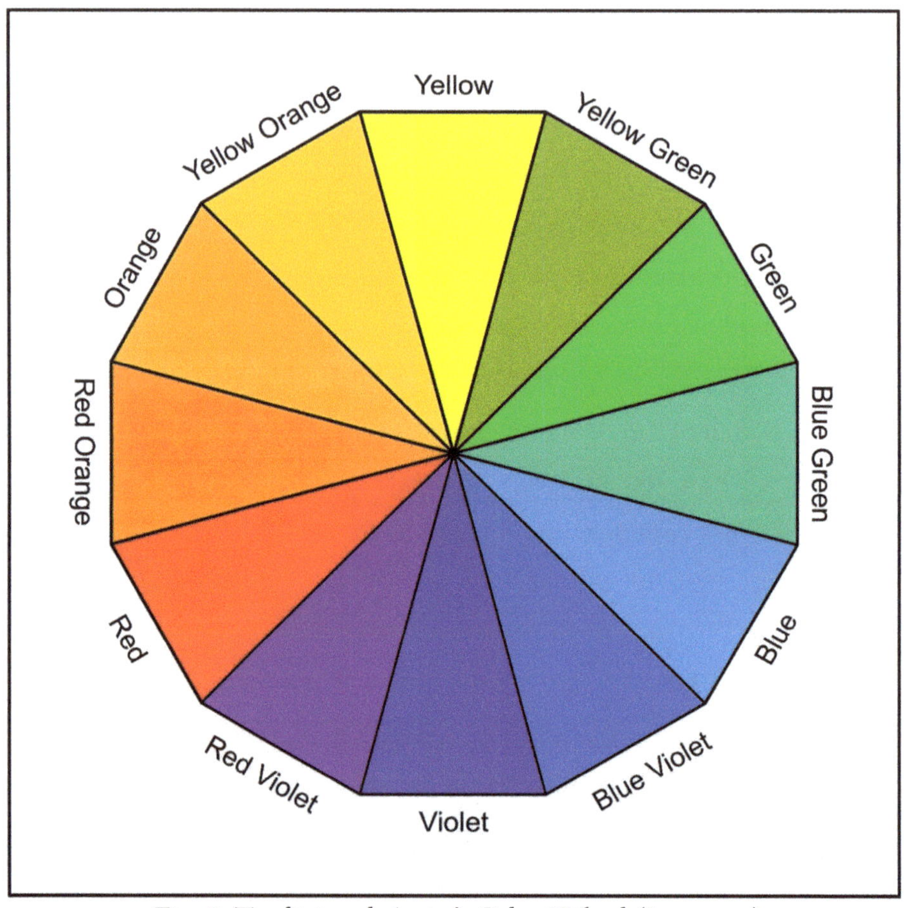

Fig. 2. Traditional Artist's Color Wheel (Incorrect)

So how do we determine the correct arrangement of colors on the color wheel? We begin with the three additive primary colors, red, green and blue. These form the foundation and basis of our color wheel. Start with red at the top, and we will call this hue 0. We will place the additive primary colors 120 degrees apart. That puts green at 120 degrees and blue at 240 degrees. Now let's place the three subtractive primaries each across from their complements. Cyan will be placed at hue 180 across from red, yellow will be placed across from blue at hue 60, and magenta will be placed at hue 300 across from green. Now we merely need to fill in the remaining six colors by mixing the two adjacent colors. At hue 30, we mix red and yellow to form yellow/red. At 90 degrees (hue 90), we mix green and yellow to form yellow/green and so on for the remaining four colors.[12]

The Solution:

This arrangement is referred to as the Holland Standardized Composite Color Wheel. I can't take credit for its discovery, but I did verify it, and it needed a name to distinguish it from the myriad of available variations. I adopted the terms "standardized" because it has been accepted as a standard by scientists, and "composite" because it contains the information required to solve color and harmony problems in both the additive and subtractive domains.[13]

---

12. In naming protocols, we generally start at the top and name things in the same direction around the wheel. When naming the tertiary colors, we use the protocol of primary-secondary. In the first example yellow is the primary and red is the secondary. So, if we call the first combination yellow-red, the second one would be called yellow-green, followed by cyan-green, and so on. In a twelve-step wheel, yellow- green is the same color as green-yellow. However, it is important to note that if there were more positions than twelve, say twenty-four, this would no longer be true.

13. This layout is accepted by science and known as the RGB color wheel. Often the colors and placement are the same but sometimes the tertiary colors are given different names. Thus, the need for standardized names, which the Holland wheel attempts to do.

When the true primary and secondary colors are placed in the correct positions on the color wheel, the result is something of mathematical beauty. Suddenly many laws of color theory and heretofore unseen relationships become readily apparent. All hues can be described by the location on a circle in degrees. Color theory problems can be solved in either the additive or subtractive domains, and color harmonies become simple geometric relationships like triangles, squares and rectangles.[14] Additionally, we now have a language with which to describe hue families and how they relate to other hues, without having to use nonsensical color names.[15] Theoretical colors can be mixed by viewing the relationship to its neighbors on the wheel and its relationship to the three primaries.

---

14. *Walter G. Holland Chroma Sutra – The Holland Lectures on Color Theory for Artists, (Lake Elsinore,CA:* Coriolis, 2025), See chapter on Color Harmony.

15. "Sky blue" is bad enough! Please don't get me started on color names. Just go to any paint store to see the nonsense. What in the world is in the opaque can of "whispering wind"?

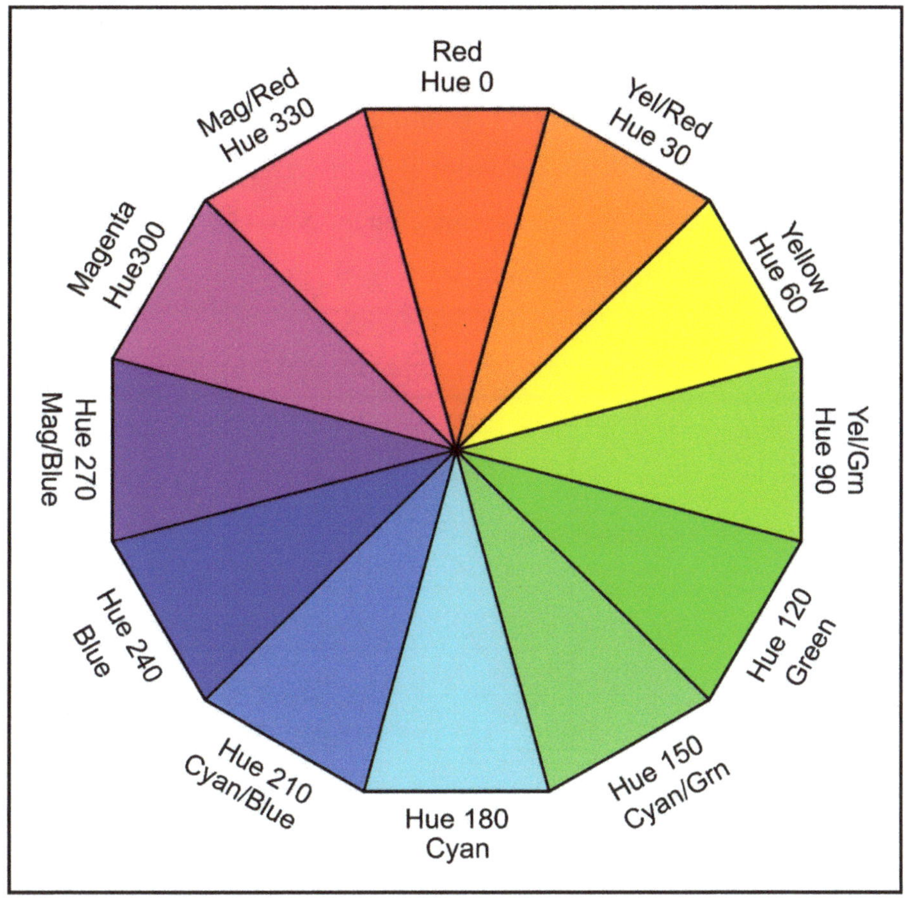

Fig. 3. Holland Standardized Composite Color Wheel

A Model for Human Color Vision Perception

As I began to put together a Grand Unified Theory of Color for Artists and Scientists, it became clear that I needed something of a functional and explanatory "Black Box" model of human color perception. I call it a "Black Box" model, since we don't really need to know the absolute workings or mechanisms of the process. We'll leave that to the highly specialized color vision scientists. We only need to understand how the system behaves and specific principles that affect artists. In a sense, it can serve as a sort of Bohr Model of the Atom, in that it is probably not fully correct technically, but will allow artists to understand the parts of perception that affect their work.

When I first started doing this research, I believed that humans had a method for discriminating individual color wavelengths in a manner similar to the way our ears discriminate pitch. Now (while still possible) I believe that function to be unnecessary.

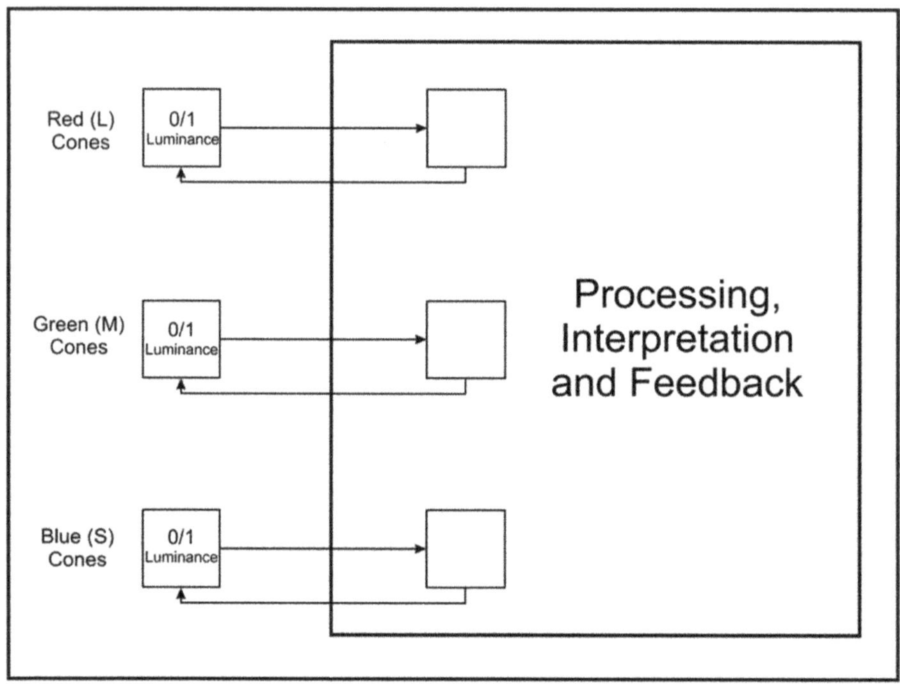

Fig. 4. Holland Black Box Model of Human Color Perception

In order to construct the Holland "Black Box" perceptual model, I made certain observations and assumptions. The first part of the system is the three types of cones, present in the fovea. In the model each of these receptors has the binary ability to detect whether or not there are wavelengths present in its individual frequency detection range and to combine that data with luminance data. The combination of this data from the three receptors allows us to see the entirety of the visible spectrum of colors.[16]

One key piece of data that moved me away from the wavelength theory of perception is the fact that there is no magenta wavelength present in the visible spectrum.[17] However, magenta is a central keystone of color theory. As it turns out, magenta is perceived by stimulating two receptors simultaneously, red and blue. Even though there is no magenta in the visible spectrum, we still clearly see it by stimulating two receptors simultaneously. In order to form the color wheel, artists take the furthest ends of the linear visible electromagnetic spectrum, red and violet, and wrap them around until the ends meet forming a circle and we call that blended region magenta.

This fact led me to speculate in about 1985, that there also likely need not be cyan or yellow in the visible spectrum. We could see cyan by simultaneously stimulating the green and blue cones, and we could see yellow by simultaneously stimulating the green and red cones. Now, no one disputes that there are many wavelengths in the visible spectrum, but this suggests that we could see the entire visible spectrum even if there were only three

---

16. In *Chroma Sutra*, I state that I am not sure where the color brightness or magnitude data comes from, whether it is from the cones or elsewhere. I'm not even sure that the idea of a binary flag for presence of receptor data is necessary but stated that if I was designing a similar system, I would certainly add it. In addition, the understanding of these details is not important for artists.

17. Fred W. Billmeyer, Jr. and Max Saltzman *Principles of Color Technology, 2nd Edition* (New York: John Wiley and Sons, 1981) Page 4.

single wavelengths present. Fifty years after I first speculated this, we now have modern LED monitors that do just that.

When one looks at an LED television or computer monitor, we see full spectrum color. However, only three wavelengths (or sometimes narrow bands) are produced. Blue is produced at about 464 nm, green at about 549 nm and red at about 612 nm. The wavelengths are carefully selected to produce the maximum color gamut, and they are also selected to be near the peak power of human sensitivity and the area of least overlap of the three cone ranges. The fact that these devices work confirms that the great majority of the wavelengths of the visible spectrum are simply not required for human color vision perception.

The next part of the Holland "Black Box" model assumes that the entire perceptual mechanism behaves like a precision measuring device, that comes to rest and prefers to stay in a state of equilibrium. So, for the first part, the precision measurement portion, we have described how the cones and other parts of the visual perception system have the ability to generate millions of colors from only three wavelengths. It accomplishes this feat by measuring proportions of the three primary colors.

Now let's look at the equilibrium portion. One very peculiar observation about color vision is that if all three receptors are stimulated equally, color information seems to disappear. As counterintuitive as this sounds, it seems to be true in both the additive and subtractive domains. In the additive domain, if you combine two complementary or three primary color light sources at the same illumination level, the result always falls on a gray scale from black to white. For example: if you mix red and blue light, by varying the luminance of both together, you will generate a color ranging from very dim magenta to very bright magenta. By varying the luminance of both independently you will generate a color from blue to red with magenta in the middle. As soon as you add green light to the magenta, the mixture turns to white, thereby losing all color information. The same is true in the subtractive domain: mix any two complementary hues and the result is black.[18] If you vary the values, the result will still fall on a neutral gray scale. Try it yourself with quality paint; or using a computer color mixing program, see what happens whenever the RGB or CMY values are equal. The color information disappears, and we are left with grayscale information only.[19]

Color Opponency and Forbidden Colors

One concept historically considered is the idea of color opponency.[20] This idea states that you can't see yellow and blue in the same place at the same time. There is also speculation about red-green color opponency. It occurred to me that perhaps if red-green opponency exists, it may be a semantic problem and should be green-magenta opponency. This is a mistake that Itten made with his afterimage testing and that led to color theory confusion. With the blue-yellow opponency you have the blue receptor and then a pair of receptors responsible for the opponent color. By changing it to green-magenta you would maintain the same relationship

---

18. Requires high quality, single pigment colors.

19. This information can be easily replicated in the additive domain by using RGB light sources, RGB computer monitors or in the subtractive domain using high quality pigments.

20. Vincent A. Billock, Brian H. Tsou. Scientific American Feb. 1, 2010. "Impossible" Colors: See Hues That Can't Exist". In 1872 German physiologist Ewald Hering suggested that color vision was based on opponency between red and green and between yellow and blue.

with the hardware. This may also predict that there should be a third cyan-red opponency.[21]

In the Holland "Black Box" model, there is no need for the concept of color opponency. Take the blue-yellow channel; we know that we can mix any color between blue and yellow. At one end of the scale you get yellowish blues and on the other end you get blueish yellows. However, if you mix equal amounts of the two colors using quality pigments, you will get black. And in fact, many of the colors in between the two ends will read as somewhat neutral grays either tending towards blue or yellow. The exact same phenomenon occurs in the additive domain, except the result in the middle is neutral gray (or white depending on illumination levels) instead of black. So, although many may not have language to describe these colors, I do believe this makes perfect sense according to color theory. Therefore, in the Holland "Black Box" model, there is no need for color opponency or forbidden colors (Forbidden colors are those that opponency theory implies shouldn't exist, like blueish-yellow), because any time you stimulate the three receptors equally (like with yellow and blue) the color information disappears anyway. This may, however, suggest a form of automatic opponency whenever the three cone stimulus values are equal.[22]

---

21. Concept not important to artists, since Black Box Model doesn't require opponency.

22. With regard to forbidden colors like yellowish-blue, when mixing paints, Holland teaches his students to always check their mix in terms of the three primaries. Is the blue you are mixing too cyan, too magenta or too yellow? It isn't that difficult to tell.

Afterimages and Self-Luminosity

Afterimages are a peculiar phenomenon that have been used historically to determine complementary colors and therefore location of colors on the color wheel. If you stare at a green square on a piece of paper, and then stare at a blank piece of paper, you will see a magenta square that may appear brighter than the original green sample or even the white paper. This phenomenon has been referred to as "self-luminosity."[23]

In the Holland Black Box Model this is explained by the almost servo-like feedback paths to the receptors. I believe that as the green square swings the green receptors to full tilt, the two remaining receptors self-generate signals to try to drive the entire mechanism back to equilibrium. If the blue and the red cones which have no stimulation are both driven with information generated by the servo system, the result would be the perception of magenta, which is the complement to green. In addition, it is possible that since the information is two receptors to one against the green, (that is to say twice as much red plus blue magnitude data) the perceived brightness of the magenta could be greater than the original stimulation (green).[24]

---

23. Self-luminous colors are seen during afterimage tests and often reported as brighter than the original stimulus. In the Holland Black Box Model, these colors are attributed to the servo-like feedback process of the perceptual apparatus.

24. The concept of this servo-driven (self-generated sensation) is not unlike the feeling of phantom limbs, which is commonly reported. In a servo system, feedback is self-generated to constantly correct the mechanism and restore it to equilibrium.

There is another interesting phenomenon that seems to lend credence to the equilibrium theory. As it happens, color harmonies that people find pleasing are always colors that when combined in the visual field, produce a neutral gray. All color schemes work this way; whether it is a simple complementary pair of colors or a complex tetradic harmony, the result is always equal stimulation of the three primary receptors. A field of yellow and blue equally stimulates R, G, and B cones. So does a field of red and cyan. In fact, all of our newly accepted harmonic formulas result in equal stimulation of all three receptors. The colors need not be combined or even side by side, it just seems that they need to be present in the visual field in roughly equal proportion.[25]

Derivation of Holland's Laws of Color Theory for Artists

The Law: Holland's Law of Primary Complements

This is a simple rule that states that if you want to know the complementary color to any primary in either the additive or subtractive domain, one simply mixes the remaining two primaries. For example, if you are mixing paint and you want to know the complement of cyan, simply mix magenta and yellow which results in red, which is the complement of cyan. If you are mixing light and you want to know the complement of green, simply mix red and blue resulting in magenta, which is green's complement.

Derivation:

Once the primary colors for both systems were determined (corrected) the law became quite apparent to one skilled in the art. If one picks any primary color, in either the additive or subtractive domain, adding the two

---

25. Ewald Hering alluded to this phenomenon of equilibrium in the late 1800s. See note 3, Itten page 20.

remaining primaries creates the complementary color. This wasn't noticed historically because of the incorrect placement of colors on the wheel, and due to the incorrect assumptions about color complements.[26]

The Law: Holland's Law of Reflection and Absorption

This is a two-part rule, relating to human (mis)perception of color. The first part says that when an object reflects all the light that it is being illuminated with, we perceive it as white. The second part is that when an object absorbs all the light it is being illuminated with, we perceive it as black. These rules are true for the most part, without regard to the actual color of the object.[27]

Derivation:

This law was hypothesized and then proven experimentally. The conclusion demonstrates that it is likely a function of our brain trying to make sense of the information it receives. Since we have no absolute color point of reference, our brain can easily be fooled into misperception of color. Imagine you have a pure red ball in a dark room. Under red light, it would appear white, since it reflects red wavelengths, and therefore all of the illumination. The same red ball under blue light would appear black, since the red pigment absorbs all of the blue wavelengths and therefore all of the illumination.

---

26. This law became plainly apparent to one skilled in the art after the correct primary colors were determined and selected.

27. This law is not universally important to all artists, however people that work in dark environments and with light generating art should understand misperception as well as perception. This also underlines the importance of full color spectrum illumination and CRI.

The Law: Holland's Law of Value Addition

In the additive domain, adding two colors should yield a lighter resultant value. In the subtractive domain, adding two colors should yield a darker resultant value. This is a law that applies equally to both the additive and subtractive domains, with inverted results.

Derivation:

This law was hypothesized and then proven experimentally. One of the discrepancies that necessitated this research was that theory suggests, in the additive domain, adding two colors should always result in a lighter value whereas in the subtractive domain, adding two colors should always result in a darker value. This makes sense; adding light together results in more light reaching the eye, whereas mixing two pigments results in less light reaching the eye. The problem is that often, due to inferior pigments, the results don't always match expectations.

One particularly problematic area is inexpensive yellow paint, that is, paint containing poor quality or multiple pigments, extenders, diluents and so on. Let's look at the example of mixing yellow and blue pigment. Theory states that mixing equal amounts of yellow and blue pigment should yield black. However, in practice, the result is often green, and sometimes lighter than the original blue pigment. This of course violates two parts of the anticipated color theory. In a theoretically ideal world, blue pigment would absorb all wavelengths except blue, which it would reflect. Yellow pigment would absorb all wavelengths except yellow, which it would reflect. Adding the yellow pigment to the blue should absorb most of the blue and yellow wavelengths leaving little light to reach our eyes and therefore appearing to be black.

The answer lies in the spectral response curves of the inexpensive yellow pigments. A high-quality pigment would reflect only yellow wavelengths, and when mixed with blue will yield black. However, an inexpensive pigment might reflect only red and green wavelengths, which would still appear yellow to our eyes, but could wreak havoc on our color theory. Even cheaper pigments might reflect everything from red to blue green, which may appear yellow to our eyes, but is roughly equivalent to adding white to the mixture, accounting for the lighter value and the lack of black.

This line of inquiry uncovered an additional area of discovery. It appears that single pigment paints are far preferable to paints that contain two or more pigments, for the study of color theory. Some inexpensive paints might contain four or five pigments combined. Mixing paints is also an experiment in chemistry. If you mix three tubes that contain four chemical pigments each, you are practically begging for unexpected results. These unexpected results could manifest themselves as toxic fumes, mutant colors, fugitive colors or even paint that never dries. If you are exploring color theory, the use of single pigment paints is highly recommended, in order to get predictable, textbook results.

Conclusion

In conclusion, it appears that Holland's laws, color wheel and general color theory, which may at first appear controversial, are easily verifiable. The portions that may seem contrary to accepted information commonly taught in art academia are in fact sound and empirically verifiable science. Upon examination I found the work to be in accordance with all currently accepted scientific research on the topic.

Additional Illustrations:

In order to use the afterimage tests, stare at the white target in the colored square for about 30 seconds and then stare at the black target in the white square to see the afterimage color.

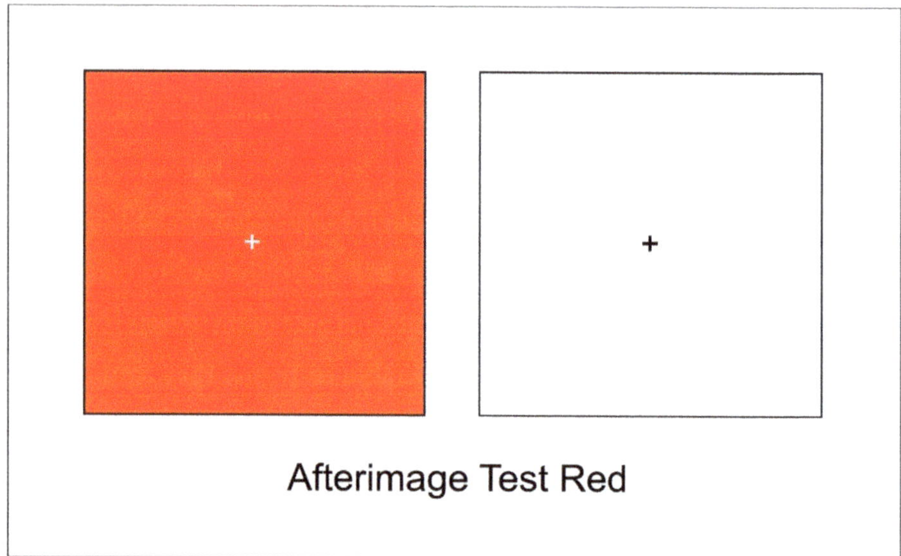

Fig. 5. Afterimage Test (Red/Cyan)

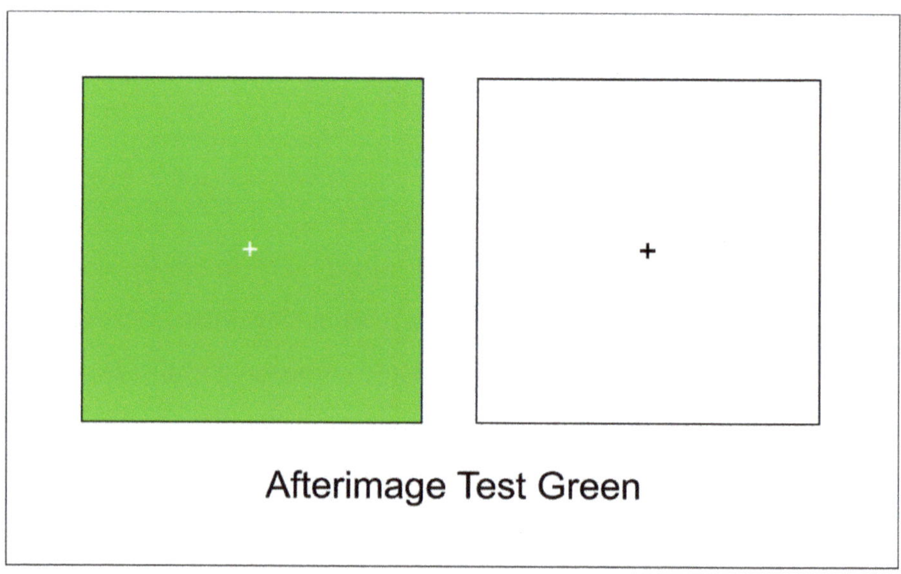

Fig. 6. Afterimage Test (Green/Magenta)

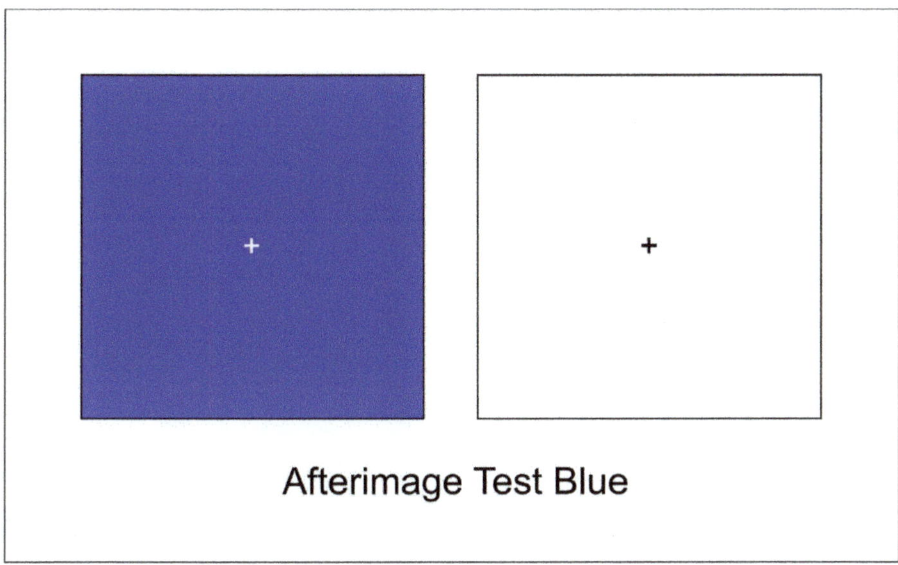

Fig. 7. Afterimage Test (Blue/Yellow)

CHROMA SUTRA

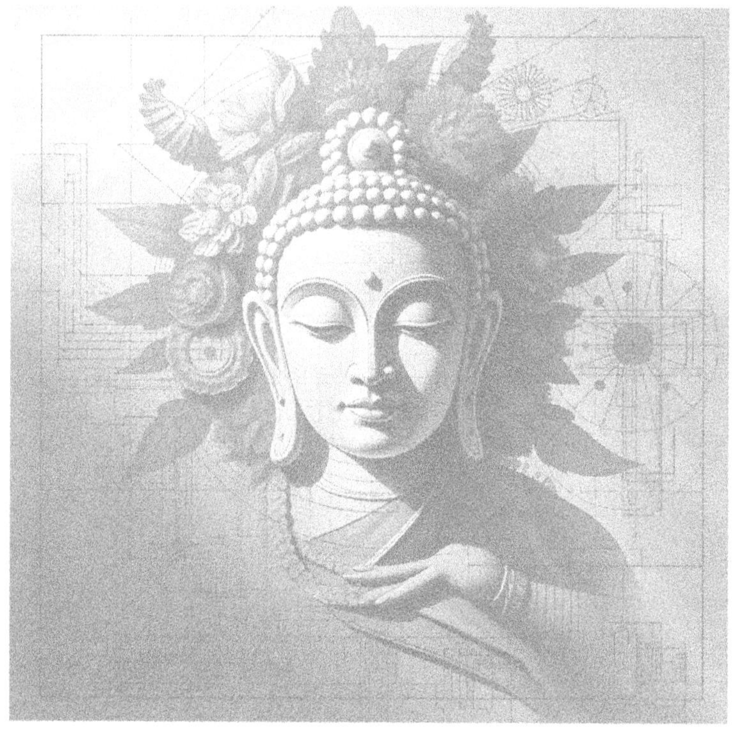

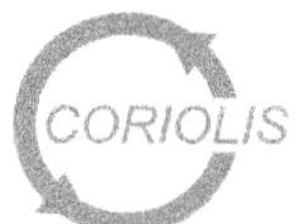

Glossary

Additive Primary Colors – The additive primary colors consist of red, green and blue. These primaries are used for processes involving the mixing of light. These are the primary colors that the eyes are sensitive to. They are called additive, because when they combine, the majority of the light eventually reaches our eyes. All mixes resulting from these primaries are lighter than the primaries themselves, since light is being added. The more light added, the lighter the mix (closer to white).

Afterimage – Afterimage is a common perceptual term that refers to an image one sees after looking at something else. One example is what do you see when you look at something and then close your eyes? In color theory, the concept of afterimage was used to figure out the complementary colors. If you stare at a blue square on a piece of paper, for example, you will then see a yellow square if you stare at a blank sheet or close your eyes.

Analogous Color Harmony – An analogous color harmony consists of two colors that are next to each other on the color wheel.

Blue – One of the additive primary colors. Blue falls halfway between cyan and magenta on the color wheel, and in the subtractive system it is mixed by adding cyan and magenta.

CMYK System – The CMYK system is a way of describing colors in terms of the amounts of the subtractive primary colors plus the addition of Black (K). This is generally used for the printing industry, but sometimes you will see it on computers as CMYK values for a particular color. This is normally expressed as a number from 0 to 100% for each component. Pure red would be C0%/M100%/Y100%/K0%. Pure white would be C0%/M0%/Y0%/K0%. Pure black would be C0%/M0%/Y0%/K100%. There is also a super black called "Rich" black which is C100%/M100%/Y100%/K100%.

Color Cylinder – See Color Space

Color Discrimination – Color discrimination is the viewers ability to tell the difference between two colors. Some viewers can only see the difference between say a few hundred colors, and some trained colorists can discriminate nearly 17 million colors. I would also note that the ability to discriminate colors can easily be learned and improved.

Color Space – A two or three dimensional model that represents the entire gamut of colors in the system you are working with. For painters, it seems practical to use a model such as a color cylinder. With a cylinder, you could divide the circumference into twelve sections to represent hue. From the outside circumference to the axis of the cylinder, you could divide the circle into fifty rings to represent saturation, with pure hue on the outside and gray at the axis. You could then slice the cylinder into fifty slices to represent value, with the top slice being white and the bottom slice being black. Even with this relatively small number of divisions, you could represent thirty thousand different paint colors.

Color Wheel – A color wheel is a method of displaying the major hues in a way that shows the harmonic relationships. In a standard color wheel, we have Red at the top labeled Hue 0. Cyan is at the bottom and labeled Hue 180. The position on the wheel is marked as the degrees of a circle. It is constructed by taking the linear spectrum and wrapping it in a circle so that the beginning and end (Red and Violet) meet to form Magenta. Magenta is a color that is not present in the form of a pure spectral wavelength, however we perceive it by mixing red and blue light.

Complementary Colors – Complementary colors are two colors that when combined form a neutral gray. Complementary colors also form a neutral gray, when combined in the mind, when they are placed in proximity to each other. The term complementary color takes into account Hue, Saturation and Value, as opposed to just Hue information.

Complementary Hues – Complementary hues are two pure hues that when combined form a neutral gray, at one end or the other of the value scale. In the additive system white is formed. In the subtractive system black is formed. The term complementary hues does not take into account Saturation and Value, as opposed to the term complementary color.

Composite Color Wheel – (Or Holland Standard Composite Color Wheel) This is a name I have assigned to the new standard color wheel that we have developed from information combining both the additive and subtractive color systems. Since it contains all of the information from both systems, it can be used to solve problems in both systems and can be used as a universal color harmony tool. (See Figure 12).

Cones – The cones are specialized receptors located in the retina of the eye (fovea) that respond to stimulation by red, green and blue light. All colors can be perceived by varying the amount of these three primary colors of light.

Computer Color Assistant – Computer Color Assistant is the name of a file I developed to help students with color harmony problems. The description for making your own can be found in Chapter 10 of this book.

Contrast – Contrast refers to the difference between two colors. The contrast can be qualitative or quantitative. We can have contrasts of hue, contrasts of saturation or contrasts of value. There can be contrasts between warm and cool colors. Contrasts are one of the fundamental elements of all design.

CRI or Color Rendering Index – The CRI is a complex measurement of how accurately a particular light source is able to render color. It measures the ability to render objects faithfully in comparison with a natural or standard light source. The scale ranges from 0 to 100 (although some sources are so poor that they have been assigned negative values), with 100 being the best. Artists should always use illumination with a CRI of 95 to 100 if practical.

Cyan – One of the subtractive primary colors. Cyan falls halfway between blue and green on the color wheel, and in the additive system it is mixed by adding blue and green.

Dyadic Color Harmony – A Dyadic color harmony is one that uses two colors. Dyad means pair. A Dyadic color harmony can be analogous, complementary or any other pairing.

Electromagnetic Spectrum – The electromagnetic spectrum is the continuum of electromagnetic radiation, organized by frequency or wavelength. The spectrum is divided into separate bands, with different names for each band. From low frequency (longer waves) to high frequency (shorter waves) are radio waves, microwaves, infrared, visible light, ultraviolet, x-rays and gamma rays.

Equilateral Triadic Harmony – An equilateral Triadic Harmony is a form of triadic harmony where you start with the key color, and instead of selecting the complement (directly across the color wheel) you select the other two colors, so that each color is 120 degrees apart. It means that the triangle has three legs the same length. This creates a pleasing harmony that also forms neutral gray in the eye / brain perception.

Fovea – The fovea is an area at the back of the retina in the eye, which contains the color receptors called cones. These cells are primarily responsible for our ability to see color.

Gamut – In color science, gamut refers to the limit of the number of colors produced by a particular system. It represents the extremes and the total. For example, a color printer can only produce a particular gamut of colors. This is also true for a display device, such as a monitor or television, or our three primary colors of paint.

Green – One of the additive primary colors. Green falls halfway between yellow and cyan on the color wheel, and in the subtractive system it is mixed by adding yellow and cyan.

Holland Ten Color Palette – The Holland Ten Color Palette is an artist's palette I have put together to optimize the tri-color mixing process for artists that paint regularly. The palette consists of Magenta, Cadmium Red Medium, Yellow Ochre, Cadmium Yellow Deep, Thalo Blue Green, Prussian Blue, Burnt Umber, Mars Black and Titanium White and Sludge Bistre.

Holland's Law of Primary Complements – This is a simple rule that states that if you want to know the complementary color of any primary in either the additive or subtractive system simply mix the remaining two primaries. For example, if you are mixing paint and you want to know the complement of cyan, simply mix magenta and yellow which results in red, which is the complement. If you are mixing light and you want to know the complement of green, simply mix red and blue to make magenta, which is the complement.

Holland's Law of Reflection and Absorption – This is a two part rule having to do with human perception of color. The first part says that when an object reflects all the light that it is being illuminated with, we perceive it as white. The second part is that when an object absorbs all the light it is being illuminated with, we perceive it as black. These rules are true for the most part, without regard to the actual color of the object. This is a function of our brain trying to make sense of the information it receives. Since we have no absolute point of reference, our brain can easily be fooled into misperception of color. Imagine you have a pure red ball in a dark room. Under red light, it would appear white, under blue light it would appear black.

HSV System – The HSV system is a way of describing colors in terms of Hue, Saturation and Value. Sometimes you will see it on computers as Hue, Saturation and Lightness. This can be a very technical description with numbers representing the levels, or just verbal descriptions like primary red at full saturation, and 50% value.

Hue – Hue is the position of a color around the circumference of the color wheel. Red is at the top by convention and is assigned the number Hue 0. The other hues are just assigned numbers corresponding to their positions on the wheel clockwise measured in degrees. For example, Cyan is Hue 180 and Magenta is Hue 300. Hue is one of the qualities we use to describe and quantify a color in the HSV system.

Isosceles Triadic Harmony – An Isosceles Triadic Harmony is a form of triadic harmony where you start with the key color, and instead of selecting the complement (directly across the color wheel) you select the two colors on both sides of the complement. Also called a Split Complementary. It means that the triangle has two legs the same length and one that is shorter. This creates a pleasing harmony that also forms neutral gray in the eye / brain perception.

Illumination – Illumination is the light source that allows us to perceive color. It can be the sun or a lamp or a specialized source of light. It can be well balanced spectrally; in which case we refer to it as a "White light source". If the spectrum is significantly distorted, it will greatly affect our ability to perceive colors accurately. One of the three basic elements of color perception.

Indigo – Indigo is a spectral color between blue and violet. I'm not a fan of the term. You will see it often in older color texts, but modern scientists find the term useless.

Magenta – One of the subtractive primary colors. Magenta falls halfway between blue and red on the color wheel, and in the additive system it is mixed by adding blue and red. One curious note: there is no pure magenta in the spectrum of sunlight. We perceive magenta because our eyes are receiving equal amounts of red and blue light.

Neutral Gray – Neutral gray can be described as any color on the scale between black and white. Neutral colors do not lean towards any of the primary colors, that is to say, they always contain exactly equal amounts of the three primary colors. (Free tip: If you are a colorist, buy sunglasses that are neutral gray. Any other type will distort your color perception).

Object – An object is something that we view under illumination. It can be a work of art or a field of grass or a painting in a museum. It can also refer to a mixture of paint on a palette or some other sample of color. One of the three basic elements of color perception.

Observer – An observer is either a person or measuring instrument that is required to perceive or quantify the color sample. One of the three basic elements of color perception.

Painter's Primary Colors – The subtractive painter's primary colors consist of red, yellow and blue. These primaries are the ones that are taught to students in school and should be forgotten immediately since they are useless.

Primary Color – A primary color is one of the three basic building blocks in a color system. It cannot be divided down further into smaller component parts. It should also be related to the three color receptors possessed by humans. Given the three primary colors, all other colors, (secondaries and tertiaries) can be generated from them. In the additive system (used for light) the primary colors are Red, Green and Blue. In the subtractive system (used for pigment) the primary colors are Cyan, Magenta and Yellow.

Primary Yellow – One of the subtractive primary colors. Yellow falls halfway between red and green on the color wheel, and in the additive system it is mixed by adding red and green.

Red – One of the additive primary colors. Red falls halfway between yellow and magenta on the color wheel, and in the subtractive system it is mixed by adding yellow and magenta.

Retinal Retention – A phenomenon also known as persistence of vision, refers to an effect in which the retina of the eye was thought to retain an image for about one tenth of a second. It is now believed that the effect may in fact occur in the brain and not the retina.

RGB System – The RGB system is a way of describing colors in terms of the amounts of the additive primary colors. This is generally used for light, but sometimes you will see it on computers as RGB values for a particular color. This is normally expressed as a number from 0 to 255 for each component. Pure red would be R255/G0/B0. Pure white would be R255/G255/B255.

Saturation – Saturation is a measure of how much of the pure hue exists in a mixture and how gray is the mix. As a color moves along a line from pure hue to pure neutral gray, we say the color is becoming less saturated. All colors at 0 saturation are neutral gray, that is there is no longer any trace of color to determine hue. Saturation is one of the qualities we use to describe and quantify a color in the HSV system.

Secondary Color – A secondary color occurs when you mix two primary colors together. As an example, in the subtractive system, you mix magenta and yellow to create red.

Shades – Shades are created anytime you add black to a pure hue. Imagine a linear scale with the pure hue (like red, for example) at one end, and black at the other. We start with the pure red and add a tiny bit of black, then more and more until the final color is pure black. Blackish red would be somewhere near the red end of the scale. Reddish black would be somewhere near the black end of the scale. In the middle would be halfway between black and red.

Sludge Bistre – Sludge bistre is a term artists use to describe the sludge at the bottom of the paint thinner can, after cleaning your brushes. After a while, the sludge becomes a nice neutral gray and historically has been used by artists to gray down the pure hues to create tones. (I just save the unused paint from my palette, and stir it up and put it in empty tubes).

Split Complementary Colors – Split Complementaries are a form of triadic harmony where you start with the key color, and instead of selecting the complement (directly across the color wheel) you select the two colors on either side of the complement. This creates a pleasing harmony that also forms neutral gray in the eye / brain perception.

Subtractive Primary Colors – The subtractive primary colors consist of cyan, magenta and yellow. These primaries are used for processes involving paint and pigment mixing. These are the primary colors that artists use. They are called subtractive, because they absorb the majority of the light that strikes them and only reflect one or more wavelengths that eventually reach our eyes. All mixes resulting from these primaries are darker than the primaries themselves, since light is being subtracted.

Tertiary Color – A tertiary color occurs when you mix a primary and a secondary color together. As an example, in the subtractive system, you mix magenta (primary) and red (secondary) to create magenta red (tertiary). I don't spend a lot of time on tertiary colors, because as a colorist you will find that virtually all colors will be combinations of the three primary colors, in some proportions, making them tertiaries. (Unless you specifically add white which puts it in a different classification. Or gray. Oh yeah, or black) See what I mean about the term not being too useful?

Tetradic Color Harmony – A tetradic color harmony consists of a key color and three other colors spaced around the color wheel. They can either be a square tetradic harmony, or a rectangular tetradic harmony.

Three Basic Elements of Color Perception – The three things required for color perception are Illumination, Object and Observer. A change to any one of these will alter the perception of color.

Tinting Strength – Tinting strength refers to the ability of a pigment or colorant to impart its effect on the color one is mixing. In other words, how strong is the pigment? For example, when using cyan, magenta and yellow, cyan is by far the color with the most tinting strength. In order to mix a tint halfway between cyan and white, one may need to add about ten time as much white as cyan. Magenta is the next strongest, but perhaps less than half as strong as cyan. Yellow is by far the weakest. When we talk about mixing colors, we often say mix these two half and half to get a color halfway in between. But that doesn't take into account tinting strength, which varies with the primaries you are using. You will get used to this effect very quickly, but always use your eyes to measure, and start by adding tiny amounts of any pigment with a strong tinting strength and constantly check the final color.

Tints – Tints are created anytime you add white to a pure hue. Imagine a linear scale with the pure hue (like red, for example) at one end, and white at the other. We start with the pure red and add a tiny bit of white, then more and more until the final color is pure white. Light pink would be somewhere near the white end of the scale.

Tones – Tones are created anytime you add neutral gray to a pure hue. Imagine a linear scale with the pure hue (like red, for example) at one end, and neutral gray at the other. We start with the pure red and add a tiny bit of neutral gray, then more and more until the final color is pure neutral gray. Grayish red would be somewhere near the red end of the scale. Reddish gray would be somewhere near the gray end of the scale. In the middle would be halfway between gray and red.

Triadic Color Harmony – A triadic color harmony consists of a key color and two other colors equally spaced around the color wheel. See also, isosceles triadic harmony, equilateral triadic harmony and split complementary harmony.

Tri-Color – Tri-color is the name of the method we use to mix colors whether it is using light, or pigments, using only three colors. For light, we use the additive primaries of Red, Green and Blue. For pigments and paint, we use the subtractive primaries of Magenta, Cyan and Yellow. (Of course, when we mix paint we inevitably need white also, in order to make tints, but "quad-color" doesn't roll off the tongue the same way). (Oh, and sometimes I just forget and call it three color).

Value – Value is a measure of how light or dark a color is as compared to a scale from black to white. As the color gets lighter, the value increases. As the color gets darker, the value decreases. Value is one of the qualities we use to describe and quantify a color in the HSV system.

Visible Light – Visible light is the portion of the electromagnetic spectrum that we concern ourselves with as visual artists. It is the portion of the spectrum that ranges from Red to Violet, that falls between Infrared and Ultraviolet. These are the wavelengths that we are able to perceive with our eyes. They range from about 380nm for violet to about 750nm for red.

Warm and Cool Colors – The terms warm and cool are very general and relative terms that describe the differences between colors. We say red, orange and yellow are the warm end of the spectrum, whereas green, blue and violet are the cool end of the spectrum. In the relative sense, even though blue is traditionally cool, we might say cyan is warmer than indigo. We might say that yellow ochre is warmer than lemon yellow.

Wavelength – Wavelength is a physical measurement of how long a wave is, from peak to peak. Light waves, being quite short, are commonly measured in nanometers. Nanometer (nm), is a unit of measure in the International System of Units (SI), equal to one billionth of a meter (0 .000000001 m).

White Light Source – White light means a source of illumination where the wavelengths of light are fairly well balanced. When all of the different colors are present in roughly equal amounts, we perceive the color of the light to be white. We call this a white light source. The sun is a white light source, in addition to incandescent lamps, fluorescent lamps and so on.

Index

CHROMA SUTRA

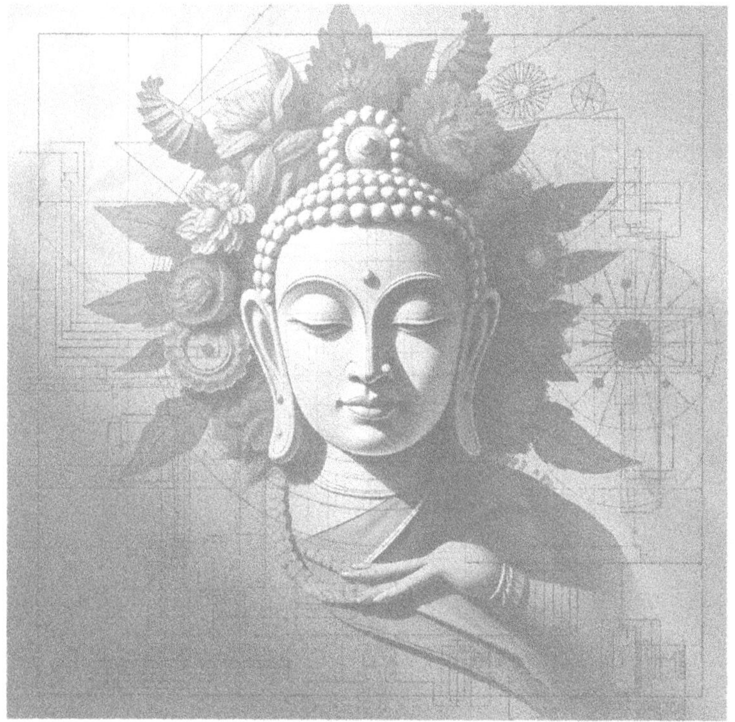

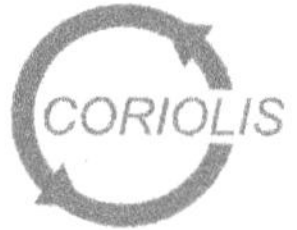

Table of Illustrations and Diagrams

CHROMA SUTRA

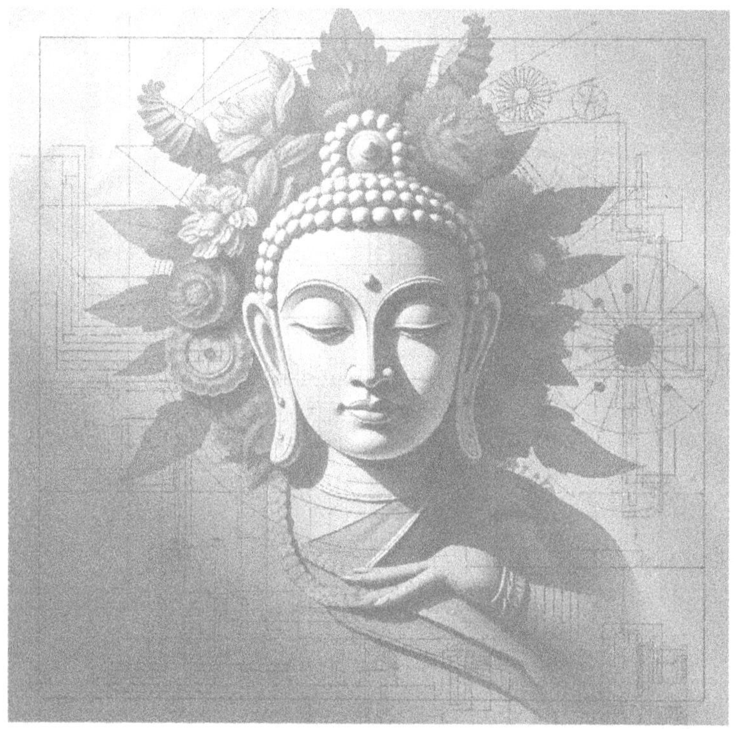

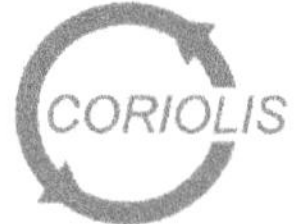

Bibliography

Albers, Joseph (1963). Interaction of Color. New Haven: Yale University Press.

Fred W. Billmeyer, Jr. (1981). *Principles of Color Technology Second Edition.* New York: John Wiley and Sons.

Chevreul, M. E. (1839). *Chevreul on the Laws of Contrast of Colour: And Their Application to the Arts.* Read & Co. Books.

Goethe, Johann. W. von (1810). *Goethe's Theory of Colour (Zur Farbenlehre). Germany.*

Harris, Moses (1766). The Natural System of Colors. England.

Itten, J. (1970). *The Elements of Color.* New York, New York: Van Nostrand Reinhold Company.

Itten, J. (1974). *The Art of Color: The Subjective Experience and Objective Rationale of Color.* New York: Wiley.

Le Blon, J. C. (1725). *Coloritto.* France.

Munsell, Albert Henry (1915). Atlas of the Munsell Color System. Malden, Mass.: Wadsworth, Howland.

Newton, Isaac (1704). *Opticks: or, A Treatise of the Reflexions, Refractions, Inflexions and Colours of Light.*

Ostwald, Wilhelm (1942). *Color Harmony Manual 12 Volumes.* Germany.

www.ingramcontent.com/pod-product-compliance
Lightning Source LLC
LaVergne TN
LVHW052345100826
845147LV00012B/756